AN ILLINOIS LEGACY

Gubernatorial Addresses of Adlai E. Stevenson 1949-1952

Edited by
Michael Maher

Paint Hill Press
Bloomington, Illinois
1985

ISBN   0-9615376-0-4

For E.D.S.

CONTENTS

This edition of previously unpublished speeches by Adlai Stevenson will mark the twentieth anniversary of his death in July, 1965. It is published in the hope that it will make more widely available to future students, the enduring values he represented and so ably expressed.

PREFACE

EVEN A CURSORY examination of these speeches will show why Adlai Stevenson's reputation as one of the most eloquent political voices of twentieth century America is so secure. It will also demonstrate why Illinoisans in his audiences three decades past have not forgotten his message. Twenty-five years after being welcomed to Springfield as a new bishop, William A. O'Connor could clearly recall and repeat what the new Governor had said on that occasion. It would be hard to imagine young national guardsmen at Camp McCoy training for possible duty in Korea, or even citizens at Danville listening to the Governor dedicate a state hospital for soldiers needing psychiatric care forgetting what was spoken in those simple surroundings, when a mundane occasion was linked to the larger historical currents moving through the world by one of the few men in public life equipped to put events in that perspective.

Mundane occasions are almost the definition of a Governor's public pronouncements. He is the all too obvious spokesman for the opening of a bridge or a convention of Lions. The number alone of these speeches, at least 140 during Stevenson's four year term, sometimes as often as seven a week, seems staggering for the chief executive of a state the size of Illinois. As he said, "If I were twins, I couldn't accept one tenth of the invitations I get and get any work done." That he accepted so many reflected not only his shrewd appreciation of the fact that as a Democratic Governor in a predominantly Republican state he needed to speak frequently before diverse audiences to maintain his authority with the legislature, but also the strong feeling he had about his state and his responsibility as its governor. No one who knew him, and no one who studies his career, can doubt the genuineness of his attachment to Illinois.

Some of Stevenson's best anecdotes turned on the alacrity with which he accepted invitations to speak. For wit was as much a signature of his speeches as eloquence or forthrightness. So, for example, he could tell the Civil Service Association that partisan political activity should not be a bar to government service, that the purpose of political parties should be to get more people active in politics, "for men and measures" rather than for mere jobs, or warn a commencement audience at Western State Teacher's College that it would be a bad thing for too many students to go to college.

But more important than either the eloquence, the wit, or the forthrightness of Stevenson's speeches was their articulation of democratic values. Again and again in these addresses to very disparate audiences, he returned to the importance of public participation in government. Stevenson firmly believed that whatever problems presented themselves to government could be resolved by more public participation in the people's business. Thus, politics at every level, from local to international, was a struggle for men's minds, in which leaders had an obligation to present the issues lucidly in their fullest context, and citizens had a responsibility to become involved in political decisions. Ultimately, the political and personal ethical responsibilities of each individual were integrally related.

> Realists know that government is bad when the people are lazy. Idealists know that we can triumph over injustice and failure if each of us lives up to the moral and the ethical obligations of citizenship...Let no people tolerate cynicism and apathy about government. Then America will be alive, responsive, and effective, both in solving our own problems at home, and in leading the way to peace in the world.

In part, such views reflected the century old role of Stevenson's own family in Illinois politics—his great-grandfather had been a close political ally of Lincoln; his grandfather shared the Democratic ticket with Cleveland, Altgeld, and Bryan. As a boy, Stevenson himself had met Woodrow Wilson and then as a young lawyer had intermittently served in the New Deal. In a larger sense, however, the public's participation in government presented a model of democratic government to states around the world emerging from centuries of colonialism and despotism.

Stevenson's acute sense of political mission took sharper focus in the Liri Valley in Italy during the winter of 1943 where

> I read a poll that said something like two-thirds of American parents would not want a son of theirs to go into politics or serve in public office. Now this seemed to me an incongruous and intolerable thing. Here their boys were dying and in misery all about me—it was all right to fight for what you believed in, but apparently it wasn't tolerable to work for it.

In the final analysis, Stevenson's ability to inspire belief in the potential of the common citizen is the enduring legacy of hope he left to Illinois and the nation. "Trust the people, trust their good sense, their fortitude, their faith. Trust them with the facts, trust them with the great decisions."

The durability of this simple idea accounts for the relevance of theme for readers of these speeches today. Reading his remarks at the "four score and seven year" anniversary of the Gettysburg Address, the dedication of a juvenile correction center, or the centenary of Nauvoo, we find ourselves thinking beyond the occasion then to the larger issues still familiar today—political refugees, East-West relations, and human rights. For all of the problems of his day, he proposed the application of those principles and methods of democratic government whose effectiveness and utility had been demonstrated through centuries of struggle and evolution. Attempts to evade or suspend those principles served neither our immediate needs, nor our long term hopes. It is one of the happy paradoxes of American political thought that such liberal ideals can be grounded in such a conservative and pragmatic conviction: democracy is the best system of government because it works better than other systems.

In the anxious years of the Cold War, darkened at home by all the suspicions and fears of McCarthyism, this message reassured Stevenson's audiences. It is a message of fortitude and hope needed today.

It may seem curious to many readers that Stevenson's gubernatorial years are relatively neglected by Illinois historians. This is the more curious because the public at the time clearly recognized his distinctiveness. He presided over what is arguably the most pathbreaking series of reforms in modern Illinois history since the administration of Governor Lowden during the First World War. During his term the ground was laid for the passage of the Gateway Amendment by which the outdated Illinois Constitution could be revised. Welfare and social service agencies were reorganized, and the various state departments, particularly the state police, were delivered from the worst abuses of patronage control.

His administration lacked the social unrest, and domestic crises, the sense of climax and volatility upon which so much of local history thrives. But if the post-war period was free of such crises, nevertheless offered the opportunity to restate and redefine the meaning of democratic government in the new post-war world. And this Stevenson did.

Few citizens could have been better equipped for this task than Adlai Stevenson, who brought a range of experiences to the office that would be enviable in a politician at the highest levels of government today. As a college student and through his Law School years, Stevenson worked during the summers as a reporter for the Bloomington *Pantagraph*. As a young attorney on LaSalle Street, he saw the whole spectrum of life in Chicago from his North Shore society friends to the corporate barons his firm occasionally represented, to the stalwarts of the city's Democratic "Organization."

In the first year of the New Deal, he went to Washington to work in the

Department of Agriculture, then returned to law in Chicago and served as President of the Chicago Council on Foreign Relations in the late thirties. He led the fight against Isolationism in Chicago as chairman of the local chapter of the Committee to Defend America by Aid to the Allies in 1940-41. He served in Europe and the Pacific as special assistant to the Secretary of the Navy until 1944, and then transferred to the State Department where he worked on the organization of the United Nations. No Governor of Illinois before or since has had the breadth of experience that Stevenson brought to his office. He also had the advantage of being a Democratic governor when that party was at the height of its national power, having controlled the Presidency and the Congress for twenty years. The optimistic and constructive perspective found throughout these speeches reflects the power which both his party and the nation had in the late 40's.

A word about the process of selection. Of the 140 speeches I have been able to identify by Governor Stevenson during his governorship, thirty were published in volume three of *The Papers of Adlai E. Stevenson*, edited by Walter Johnson. In choosing the thirty-seven addresses reprinted in this volume, I have tried to represent the breadth of audiences Stevenson's governorship touched, and the wide range of his speaking style, which was always adapted to a particular audience. He could speak almost informally to a summer festival audience, rouse a partisan audience with a spirited stump speech, talk more soberly to the national guardsmen at Camp McCoy, or speak in his most official voice addressing the state legislature or national conferences—and always remain distinctively Stevenson.

I should also have preferred to include more of the Governor's addresses to the Illinois Legislature, or his periodic radio reports to the people in order to make them more widely available for the historical record. However, it was clear that their detailed treatment of highway problems, tax issues, and the host of social service matters that are the daily business of state government would only weary most readers. For the same reason, I have deleted some sections from the speeches reprinted below. I have emphasized those speeches that show Stevenson's eloquence and humanity to best advantage. For this was the point of curiosity that first drew me to his gubernatorial speeches more than a decade ago.

1949

I AM GOING TO speak to you briefly about the Constitutional Convention proposal which is pending before the General Assembly in Springfield. There are more entertaining subjects we might discuss this evening. A simple, unadorned travelogue, entitled "journeys in the jungle of politics, or why Illinois Governors age so rapidly" would be more interesting. But right now, I must put aside more diverting topics and stick to the most important legislative business before the people of Illinois.

A question which frequently arises in connection with Constitutional revision is this: "Why a Convention? Aren't we getting along all right under our present Constitution?" The answer to that question is clear. We don't get along at all under our Constitution of 1870. We can't. We get along under a system of adjustments which range all the way from evasion and subterfuge to downright violation.

Let me illustrate: The Constitution commands that representation in the state legislature shall be in accordance with population and that the legislature shall re-district the state every ten years. It is now just short of half a century since the legislature has obeyed that flat command. During that period there have been tremendous shifts in the distribution of our population. The equality of representation which the present Constitution requires has long since disappeared. Some of you are not just "second class citizens" when it comes to voting for representatives in the State Legislature. Depending upon the legislative district in which you live, you may be tenth, or even fifteenth class citizens. By that I mean that the vote of some of our citizens have one seventh or one eighth the weight in selecting representatives to the legislature of the votes of other citizens of Illinois. Our present districts vary in population from 40,000 to 575,000.

That's but one illustration of how we get along under our 1870 Constitution. Look now at the field of taxation. The utter impossibility of uniform taxation of all kinds of property is not some newly discovered scientific truth. It is perfectly clear that intangible personal property—bonds, stocks, bank deposits and the like—cannot be taxed at the same rate which is applied to real estate. The current tax rate in Cook County is $3.17 per $100 of assessed value. The taxation of bank deposits yielding no return or bonds yielding little at that rate would be confiscatory. Yet that is what the Constitution of 1870, framed when land was the principal form of wealth, commands. Hence, of course, the post-civil war uniformity clause is regularly and consistently violated, both privately and officially. We get along under the Constitution in this instance by violation because it is impossible to get along by compliance.

Then there is the pattern of evasion by which local governments, cities, school districts, park districts, drainage districts, etc., have managed to furnish the services demanded of them in spite of the constitutional provision which limits the amount of their indebtedness to five per cent of the assessed valuation of the property within their boundaries. The technique is simple but extremely costly. Since an existing municipality is limited in the amount of indebtedness it may incur, a new municipal corporation is created whenever a new service is demanded by the people. The new municipality then has its own independent five per cent debt limit. And so municipalities have been pyramided one on top of the other in utter disregard for sound principles of governmental administration. The letter of the constitutional provision is satisfied, but it is satisfied at a heavy cost—in administrative overhead duplication, and in the greatly lengthened ballots which sharply curtail the possibility of effective control of his government by the voter.

It is probably not widely known that Article 10 of the Constitution not only freezes in detail the county officers to be elected but also specifies the maximum salaries to be paid to those officers. The salaries, of course, are fixed according to the standards of 1870. They are obviously inadequate today. As a result devices have been developed—elastic expense accounts —by which county officers receive additional compensation.

These illustrations of violations and evasions do not exhaust the list. Some of them cost us heavily in dollars; others take their toll in terms of the voter's diminished control over officials; all of them cheapen respect for law and for government. And they continue over the years to gnaw at the foundations of our institutions.

Let me read you an apt description of our situation in Illinois today.

> For years past the machinery of our state government has been kept in motion only by continued violation of plain and positive constitutional provisions. Nothing can be more pernicious. By this the people lose their respect for the laws, and learn to hold them in contempt. A reverence for constitutions and laws is the best possible guaranty for the stability of the state, the peace and good order of society, and the

protection of the life, liberty and the property of the citizen. And whenever it becomes necessary to violate a constitution, it should be changed to meet and remove the necessity which impelled to such violation.

Those are the words of the men who framed our present Illinois Constitution. In those terms they justified the convention which produced the Constitution of 1870. They are precisely applicable to our situation in Illinois today. When we lose respect for constitutional government; when we lose respect for public office and public office holders, we lose respect for democracy. It makes little difference what we preach; it is what we do that counts. I recall Emmerson's words: "Don't say things; what you are stands over you and thunders so that I cannot hear what you are saying."

The need for action to end our pattern of violations and evasions is far more urgent today than it was eighty years ago. Today the whole world is convulsed by the struggle between our ideas and ideals of government and a directly contradictory set of ideas and ideals which is highly distasteful to us. Our shortcomings, which yesterday were local in their impact, are today exploited around the world.

Now let's look for a moment at the major arguments against the Constitutional Convention. One of them is that a sufficient case has not been made out to justify the need for a convention. I have tried to look at that objectively and I can't make much sense out of it. The reapportionment required by the present Constitution has been cynically disregarded for generations. Realistically, I think there is going to be no reapportionment until a method is devised which will effect a compromise between population and geography as a basis for representation in the two Houses of the state legislature. Successful illustrations of that kind of compromise are all about us—the most notable being the United States Senate which is elected on a geographical basis and the House of Representatives which is chosen on a population basis.

Our present Revenue Article compels individual and official violations of the Constitution. That state of affairs is going to continue until classification of property for tax purposes is permitted by the Constitution.

Turning to the Judiciary Article of the Constitution, much of the time and energy of the Supreme Court is occupied by cases which come before it not because of their importance today, but just because they were significant to the land economy which prevailed when the Constitution of 1870 was adopted. And so the judges find themselves unable to consider many matters of great economic and social significance in today's industrial and commercial economy.

Cook County today has more than half the population of the state. And yet under the present Constitution, Cook County, where over half the cases before the Supreme Court originate, can elect no more than one of the seven judges of the Supreme Court.

I don't see how anyone could deny that these examples spell out a compelling case for a Constitutional Convention, and I have not even mentioned housing, home rule and other handicaps to efficient and effective government. If a Convention isn't clearly indicated now, I can't help wondering how much more difficult our plight must become before we can get one. Nor can I understand why some leading business people who have so much at stake in orderly, efficient, responsible public administration should persist year after year in opposing constitutional reform. They would never run their own businesses under obsolete and rigid charters and by-laws, but they insist that the biggest business of all — the public business — be conducted that way.

One reason, I'm told, is that they fear a Convention might authorize a graduated income tax. I think I have made my position clear on that subject. But lest there be any misunderstanding, let me repeat what I said in my inaugural message: "I know of no large number of our people who favor a state income tax. I know a great many who oppose it. Rather than risk the rejection of a new Constitution because of this apprehension I would urge the Convention to leave the income tax problem precisely where it stands at present." In any event the people would first have to approve the provision in the new Constitution authorizing an income tax and then at some later date the legislature would have to enact it. So at worst there would still be formidable obstacles to pass before Illinois could ever have an income tax.

Recently there has been an attempt to arouse apprehension that a Convention might scrap the Bill of Rights contained in the present Constitution. But in spite of the huffing and puffing, I doubt if many people take it seriously. And I am completely confident first, that the people of Illinois will not elect delegates who will propose any wholesale changes in the Bill of Rights, and second, that the people of Illinois would not ratify their work if they should propose such changes.

In addition to the Constitutional Convention resolution, there is also pending in Springfield a "party responsibility bill" intended to make the method of voting on the proposal to call a Convention resemble as nearly as possible the method which was used between 1870 and 1891.

After each House of the Legislature by a two-thirds vote adopts a resolution calling a Convention, the question must be submitted to the voters.

As it is now, a majority of those voting at the next general election have to approve that resolution before a Convention can be held. Please note carefully that a majority of those who vote for or against a Constitutional Convention is not enough: a majority of those who vote at the election is required. And that means that the indifferent and apathetic — those who don't vote on that issue at all — in effect are counted as voting against it.

Now that is the machinery prescribed by our present constitution and it worked satisfactorily from 1870 until 1891. But in those days each political party printed its own ballots and each party took a position for or against a constitutional proposal as it saw fit. Votes for the candidates of a political party were also votes for that party's position on the constitutional issue.During that period there was no difficulty in securing the requisite number of votes to amend our constitution.

Then in 1891 came the Australian ballot law which substituted an officially printed ballot for the party ballots which had previously been used. Right then our constitution became rigid and inflexible. The requirement which was not difficult to fulfill under the method of voting which the framers of the constitution were familiar with and which they had in mind was quite accidentally converted by the adoption of the Australian ballot act into a barrier which has proved almost insurmountable.

The purpose of party responsibility legislation is to permit each political party to take a position for or against a Constitutional Convention proposal just as they did when the Constitution was written. The position of each party will be determined in the primary election which precedes the general election. Of course an opportunity is provided so that the independent voter may freely express his own position for or against the convention.

That is the story which I wanted to tell you tonight, and what it lacks in plot and glamour and climaxes, is more than made up, I assure you, in importance to you as citizens of Illinois. I bespeak your interest in this complicated, difficult subject. It is time we decided whether we are going forward or backward in Illinois. There is no standing still.

The time has come for thinking people to think. The time has come when we must serve our great tradition greatly.

CIVIC RECEPTION FOR BISHOP O'CONNOR, SPRINGFIELD
March 17

BISHOP O'CONNOR, I know you have sensed the same warmth and sincerity in Springfield's greetings that I sensed when our Capital City welcomed me a long time ago—about two months! And I am happy and honored to join my fellow citizens tonight in extending to you the cordial welcome they so generously gave me at my inauguration.

We have something in common, Bishop O'Connor: Our administrations are commencing at about the same time. I suspect that is about as close as I will ever come to anything in common with a Bishop. But I also suspect that your administration will long outlast mine. So, in spite of my head start, I am going to concede you the victory right now.

You come, Bishop O'Connor, to our friendly, hospitable Springfield to take up the great responsibility of your distinguished and beloved predecessor and my great friend, Bishop Griffin. But you also come here to the Capital City of Illinois as the representative of a faith, a civilization and a tradition that reaches back to our beginnings. Since Marquette and Joliet passed this way, leaders of your faith have built for you, for your successor, and for all of us a great tradition of spiritual, charitable and educational service—a tradition I am confident you, Bishop O'Connor, will carry on with vigor, vision and understanding.

As director of charities in the largest Catholic Diocese in the world, your love for and your interest in young people has earned you a precious, albeit unofficial title: "The Children's Bishop." In my new position I too have an urgent concern for the young. The problems of school aid and of reducing delinquency are high on the list of questions for which we are trying to find the best possible answer.

In a very real sense there is a close relationship between the new responsibilities which Bishop O'Connor is taking upon his shoulders and those which confront me as Governor of this state. In several ways, the functions of the church, and I am referring here to all of our churches, complement the functions of state government. Both have vital interests in the field of education; both are concerned with the care of the aged and the handicapped and others in need of help. Through the churches many of these people have been able to avoid becoming public charges.

In a broader sense, the churches are a vital, unifying, spiritual force in our society without which our American democracy could never have achieved its strength and stability, and without whose continuing influence our free institutions of government would certainly disintegrate.

We live in a time of trial and challenge. In the tense struggle for peace on which rests the fate of our civilization, the force of religious faith is our hope. We need that now just as surely as our sons needed the strength of religion on the battlefield in the recent war.

We shall build neither enduring peace nor lasting prosperity unless we cling to the ideals learned in our several churches; unless we hold high those ideals in our lives, and, by our example, convince other peoples that only upon such ideals can world understanding be built.

The parallel between the fundamental teachings of the churches and the aims of our form of government may be put another way. The church teaches the dignity of man and devotion to God and country. These are likewise fundamental precepts of government as we understand it. The stamping out of slavery in every form, the protection of the dignity of man, the elimination of intolerance, and the preservation of religious freedom, all these are things to which the churches and free governments are jointly committed.

The kind of society, the kind of world which our children will inherit depends upon us, upon the example we furnish, and upon how closely we, ourselves, stand by the moral standards which past generations have handed down to us. Through the philosophy of our forefathers ran the golden thread of faith: faith in God, faith in the destiny of America, faith in the home and in the good citizenship which shapes that destiny. We need to cherish that faith in this and succeeding generations, to never lose sight of our great heritage and the priceless values of American life.

And so I say, Bishop O'Connor, that you not only have a heavy responsibility, but a great opportunity for service to your church and to all Illinois, for the advancement of education, the care of the underprivileged, and for the promotion of happier community relationships. In these tasks, which are in part my tasks, you will have the cordial cooperation of my office and of the other agencies of the state government.

JEFFERSON-JACKSON DAY DINNER, CHICAGO
April 7

O N THIS OCCASION we can well reflect a bit on why the Democratic Party is the oldest and the most successful of all the long list of American political parties that have crossed the pages of our history. This is a good time to look at some of our present day problems against the background of Jeffersonian and Jacksonian ideals and philosophy. I think we would do well to resolve to cling to those ideals in searching for the solution of those contemporary problems.

The Democratic Party has stood the test of time. Other parties have come and gone but ours goes on and on, and today I think we can say that in spite of the dissensions and divisions which seemed to threaten our very existence a few months ago, our party is stronger in terms of public confidence than ever. I pointed out at Springfield a week ago that it was no accident that the Democratic Party has won twenty-two of the thirty-eight national elections since 1800. During that time the Democratic Party has pitted itself against Federalists, Whigs, and Republicans, but it has always retained its own identity and most of the time it has held firm to its principles. And when the candidates of our party have been true to those principles we always have won.

The explanation is simple. Since the days of Jefferson and Jackson ours has been the party of the people. Most of the time the people knew our party was the one most responsive to the needs and will of the average American citizen. Sometimes, but not always, the Democratic Party happened to have the most glamorous candidates, but that was not the real secret of its success. The real secret was that by holding fast to its character as the people's party, our Party has won the allegiance of millions of independent voters.

Actually we know that political party affiliations are less prescribed today than they were in years past. No longer do men and women vote Democraťtic or Republican merely because their fathers and mothers did. We have reached political maturity. Today people more and more judge political parties and political candidates by what they stand for. And these are the voters — the voters that one can't rope and tie and brand — that decide elections. This growing discernment on the part of the voters accounts more than anything else, it seems to me, for the present fortunes of our party.

Let me put it another way. Harry Truman did not win last November because of his intrepid courage alone. He won because he was able to convince the people that his heart beat for the average American; that he was on their side, and that he would fight and keep on fighting for them.

No, the American people didn't vote for President Truman because of sentiment—they voted for him because he fought the same kind of front that Andy Jackson fought against the forces of special privilege in his day. The voters knew that the future of America was safest in the hands of a political party dedicated to the realization of their hopes and their aims. The voters understood the real issues, as Jackson made them understood in his historic fight against the concentration of the national wealth and resources in private hands. Harry Truman spoke to the pople and they heard him.

There is an important lesson in this for all of us. The people here in Chicago and in Illinois put us in office because they had confidence that we too would do the best job for them. Now it is up to us to do that job. We must not forget our pledges. We must not forget the goals we set forth for ourselves, goals the voters approved. We must keep the faith.

What are these goals? What is it that we must do to keep the faith with the voters of Illinois?

In the state administration we are striving to restore common honesty, decency and integrity in our State government.

We are seeking to place in positions of responsibility men who will discharge their duties with vision, fairness, and courage.

We are trying to give the people a fair chance to express themselves on the issue of a modern constitution for a great progressive state.

We are striving for better schools in Illinois. We recognize that the State government must assume a greater share of the cost of education. We are trying to strengthen the teaching profession and to equalize educational opportunities for every Illinois boy and girl.

We are improving law enforcement to save what remains of our roads.

We are seeking to increase respect for the civil rights of all citizens and eliminate racial discrimination in employment.

We are striving to eliminate corruption and graft wherever they have taken root. We are taking idlers off the public payrolls. We are demanding honest services from State employees and honest values in State purchases.

We are doing our best to improve the facilities and the personnel for the care of the thousands of unfortunates in our State hospitals.

We are taking politics out of the vital mine inspection service.

We are trying to put the regulation of utilities on a level of maximum competence.

We are undertaking to strengthen our labor laws, to provide better housing and better highways, and to broaden and improve our public health services.

These are some of the goals we have set and the people approved. We must never permit ourselves to forget them.

The fight will not be easy. There will be temporary set-backs along the way. We know that there always has been—and I suppose always will be—a clash for power between those who want the government to serve their selfish interests and those who want the government to serve the interest of all without any distinctions of wealth or class. But we also know that as long as we are honest in our intentions and our efforts, as long as we truly have the public interest at heart, we are on the right side and the right road, and the people will be with us.

A while ago I said that our Party enjoys a high degree of public confidence at the present time. I think that is confirmed by what happened in the local elections in Illinois last Tuesday. The victories won by Democratic candidates in so many of the local contests offer strong proof that the people are with us in this fight we are waging to reestablish the integrity and the conscience of our democracy at all governmental levels here in Illinois.

We have got to keep on playing the game according to the rules laid down by Jefferson and Jackson. We have got to keep on waging the kind of fight for the people's interest that they waged in the early days of this republic and that Franklin Roosevelt and President Truman have waged in these later days. We must rally to the united support of our own Scott Lucas, the leader of our party in the Congress, and Paul Douglas whose brief service has already commanded national attention. We have got to give the people the kind of government that Mayor Kennelly stands for here in Chicago.

Then, and only then, can we hope to retain the confidence of people. Then, and only then, will we be faithful to our trust.

And most of all we must never forget that there is strength in party unity, in common purpose, in loyalty. To divide and conquer is an ancient formula. The malicious will try to divide us, try to set downstate against Chicago, try to foment personal jealousies and ambitions.We must be wary of the tale bearers and the gossips. Our greatest hazard is disunion, suspicion, jealousy. Together we can't fail. Divided and at cross purposes we can't succeed.

INAUGURATION OF D.W. MORRIS AS PRESIDENT OF SOUTHERN ILLINOIS UNIVERSITY, CARBONDALE
May 5

ALTHOUGH ITS CURRICULUM has broadened in recent years, so that this is no longer exclusively a teacher's training institution, (Southern Illinois University) still retains teacher training as it primary objective. More than half of the students here are taking courses designed to qualify them as teachers. These men and women will, I hope, take their places in the depleted ranks of the teaching profession, and do their part in helping to rebuild that profession to the high and honored place which it formerly held and which it deserves to hold today.

If I correctly interpret the signs, there is taking place in Illinois what might be called a revolution in education. Our people are demanding better schools, from the kindergarten to the graduate colleges.

The trend toward consolidations has in a few years eliminated several thousand small, uneconomic school districts by local intitative and leadership. Curricula are improving. Teachers' salaries are rising. I have proposed a large increase in State aid to our common school system—the largest in our history. And I will have some further proposals to make regarding the distribution of this money calculated to make further progress toward a sound foundation program and proper organization of school districts in Illinois.

I do not believe the public demand for more State aid for schools stems entirely from any selfish belief that increased State appropriations will mean that local taxes will be reduced as a result. I think it stems rather from a feeling that Illinois needs to do more than it has been doing to give our boys and girls a standard of education commensurate with our wealth and our great resources.

I believe this demand has arisen in full realization that increased State aid for the schools is going to come out of the pockets of the people. Although no one likes to contemplate increased taxes, I think the people are saying that they are willing to pay higher taxes if need be to get better schools.

Two weeks ago in my budget message to the General Assembly, I recommended an increase of 70 per cent in the level of State aid to the schools. But I said then, and I repeat now, our troubles will not all be solved by voting larger amounts for the schools from the State Treasury. I stated then, and I believe few would deny, that much local and state money is being expended for inferior schools, for inadequate and shallow curricula, for mediocre direction of educational policies and school management.

I believe we must devise means whereby the State realizes a special obligation to those districts which take steps to improve their school district organization. I do not believe that we should pour more and more millions into a system which in some respects has grown obsolete and inefficient. It is my hope that in the current session of the General Assembly we will be able to write into our school laws a method whereby the increased grants of State aid which I have recommended will serve to encourage the establishment of better organized, better staffed and better equipped schools to replace many of those which are now wholly inadequate.

I make no pretense of expert judgment, but I believe we are making progress toward the improvement of the quality of teacher training. And now we must strive to interest more qualified young people in teaching as a career. With better schools, higher standards of teacher qualification, better salaries and security, I confidently believe we are on the eve of an era of increasing attractiveness in the teaching profession, which has so long been neglected.

I hope I am not wrong, because more and better teachers is certainly one of our most acute shortages, and particularly in Illinois. It will doubtless take some time to recover the lost ground, and we must try to make more of our young people aware of the sense of satisfaction, the sense of accomplishment, that goes with doing an important, necessary, basic work in a civilized community.

We know that the war's disruption of our economy left the teaching ranks critically reduced. We know that we are not now training elementary school teachers rapidly enough to meet even current needs, let alone to fill the gaps left by defections from the teaching ranks.

We know, for example, that we still have almost 2400 teachers in Illinois serving under emergency certificates, which means that they do not meet the standards of training which we have established by law. Yet these emergency teachers have stepped into a breach that could not be filled otherwise, and they have served a most useful purpose.

We have only to consider that less than one-half of the teachers now serving in Illinois have a college degree to realize that we have a serious deficiency in training in our teacher ranks. A recent study made by the State Superintendent of Public Instruction showed that 8 per cent of the 33,700 teachers in our public elementary and high schools had no training at all above the high school level, or less than one year of college work.

While our supply of new teachers has been falling below the need for some years, the trend in public school attendance has been swinging sharply higher, which points up with even greater emphasis the task ahead. We will need more teachers to staff more classrooms within the next decade, and we will need better trained teachers because in the complex and specialized society of the future the boy or girl with inadequate educational preparation will be under a tremendous handicap.

That represents a large part of the mission of this University as I see it. The remainder lies in the training which Southern is giving to the youth of this area in the College of Vocations and the College of Liberal Arts. It lies in preparing the youth of this area for service in the industries, in the professions, the cultural life and public life of this whole section. It lies in preparing them to meet the myriad tasks of the future in order that they may apply new knowledge and methods to the problems that are peculiar to southern Illinois, and ultimately to achieve a happier, fuller way of life.

In the period since this institution was founded—indeed in the last quarter century—we have come to realize more and more that the extension of education among the world's peoples is one of our best hopes for the future. Experience has taught us that greater understanding among men and nations is essential to world peace. We look primarily to education to bring about that understanding.

We know that the educational system of America cannot do the job alone. But we can set an example for the world. We can demonstrate that the American way of free education, free enterprise, free government and free opportunity is the best possible way to happy, peaceful living among ourselves and among nations. We can, we must continue to lend encouragement and support to men and women everywhere who long for emancipation from ignorance, tyranny and poverty.

In helping to preserve and foster these traditional American ideals, while pursuing with fidelity its own immediate tasks, Southern Illinois University under the leadership of President Morris will be fulfilling one of the great responsibilities of higher education in the United States. It also will be helping to build a richer Illinois and a stronger America.

ILLINOIS COLLEGE COMMENCEMENT, JACKSONVILLE
June 12

YOU DO ME GREAT honor to invite me here today to the heart of Illinois' greatest resource, her farmlands — and to Illinois College, another of our finest resources and one of the most venerable and distinguished educational institutions of our State. Jacksonville is not alone the home of three Illinois governors but the cradle of many of the great spiritual and cultural ideas which have enriched the life of Illinois. Even a Princeton graduate like myself must admit that it is an honor to commemorate the memory of the small band of Yale theological students who founded this college 119 years ago. Without their vision and courage both the educational and spiritual development of Illinois might have been long delayed.

I have noticed from considerable painful experience that oratory in the United States reaches peak production usually in June around commencement time or in October just before elections. Not infrequently commencement oratory is so lush and vaporous that the ideas, if any, are never visible at all. Sometimes commencement speakers say nothing in several thousand well chosen words, and not infrequently they blithely or piously, but always confidently, set out to revamp or alter the ideas gathered by graduates in four hard, happy years of college.

"Are commencement speakers necessary?" It's a fair question, and I haven't much doubt how you feel about it. I felt the same way on the day I sat in your place and listened to a distinguished man talk sagely about important things that were good for me to hear. But I can't remember who he was or what he said. And the only thing I say today with complete assurance is that you won't remember me or what I say either!

Of course I have a faint hope that what I say will be simple, short and some help to you, but I have little doubt that before I finish I will have committed all the conventional sins of commencement day speakers.

Because of the special position which Illinois College has had in the development of our State and in providing thoughtful, reasoning, spiritually attuned persons to lead our communities, our State and nation; because of the positions of leadership which each of you will take in your communities, I would like to consider with you an ancient problem which is more acute today than usual—what we ourselves can do as our own part in the war of ideas which is torturing our times. I said an "ancient" problem because there are always acute conflicts of ideas in the world. It is well there are; there is no better antidote for the complacency of the complacent or the resignation of the resigned. But this is and has been for a generation one of those periodic eras of social revolution out of which good or evil of long historical duration usually emerge.

There was a day when we Americans believed that it was only necessary for the rest of the world to know about democratic freedom and then they would desperately want it. We used to take it pretty much for granted that the oppressed and wretched masses of Asia, or even the primitive natives of Africa, would be yearning for the blessings of freedom and democracy. Forgetting our own stormy history and bitter struggles, in our blind faith and sometimes naive hope, we failed to recognize that words and platitudes, dreams and ideals, were not sufficient to win the interest of the hungry, oppressed and ignorant. We exported our speeches and our finished goods, but seldom offered a way for all to share in these goods or the tangible hope which would give concrete meaning to our ideas and free institutions.

But of late we have been awakening to the fact that people who have been hungry or oppressed are attracted to adroit, emphatic demagogues who offer them a blueprint of a new world without hunger and oppression. True, we know these blueprints don't disclose the price in terms of human rights and freedoms, but to the native of Burma or the coolie of China who has never enjoyed and seldom even heard of these privileges of democratic life they have scarely any meaning.

Almost too late we have learned that hope to many does not precede but follows tangible economic and social advance. So at last we are rapidly learning the facts of life and making the first beginnings of a realistic attack on the central problem of our time, which is victory in the war of ideas and peace. Now, belatedly, we are starting to export our most marketable and precious product, the "know-how" which has made this country the envy of the world and the greatest social and political force since the fall of Rome.

But don't misunderstand me. I don't intend to propose that all of you disperse to the far corners of the globe to peddle the Federalist papers or to preach democracy to the natives. Rather, I prefer to outline another and perhaps even more pressing obligation — to set our own house in order. And I want particularly to talk with you about the special responsibility which you will have in your communities. What happens in each of our communities today has a composite effect on our international relations just as much, if not just as immediately, as what the Secretary of State does in Paris or London or Washington tomorrow. I say this because to export any commodity profitably it must be marketable.

The individualist tradition, the democratic product, is saleable only if it is good, only if it works efficiently and well. To say it is good and works well isn't enough—you have to demonstrate it, prove it. But it's so large and complicated few of us understand it well. Its component parts are 155,000 governing units, school boards, conservation districts, the municipalities, states, the nation. It must be considered in terms of the 1,000,000 elected officials, from drainage district trustee to President. It must be considered in terms of the 5,770,000 full time employees who work for these governing bodies, and the $55 billion which will be spent by them during this current year. It must be considered in terms of our own state and the billion dollars of your taxes we will be spending during the next two years. But mostly this product—if it is to be marketable at all in the rest of the world—must be considered in terms of the ninety million potential voters in this country, and whether they are interested in and vigorously sharing in the responsibilities as well as the rights of democracy.

You as the future leaders in your various communities have an added responsibility to keep our own democratic machinery in motion. You above all others must know and understand our problems. Illinois had only 160,000 inhabitants in 1830 when this college was founded. Five years later at your first convocation only two students graduated. In the last forty years our national population has risen from 92 million persons to an estimated 140 million; and our State population from about five and half million to eight and three-quarter millions today. In the last two years alone Illinois has grown by 300,000. Since the war began the state population of young folk under five years of age has increased about 45 per cent and persons over sixty-five years of age by about 25 per cent which largely increases our costs because these groups are the largest consumers of public services. Have you considered what all these facts and figures mean in terms of our government, and of our obligations as citizens to make that government work and work well?

Of course these facts and figures of our phenomenal growth are in themselves insignificant as compared to their impact on our responsibilities in the world today. It is no longer enough to say "let the world roll by." A hundred years ago it took the British Ambassador as long to travel from Rome to Paris to report to Queen Victoria as it took a Roman general to travel from ancient Britain to Rome to report to his Caesar. But I could be having dinner tomorrow in Rome—were it not for a legislature busily working over my program in Springfield.

And we can no longer say that our democracy is complete if we only mouth the right words on the proper occasions. In the current war of political ideas which will last for a long, long time, what happens in each one of those 155,000 governing bodies in this country may well change or upset our influence. Every lynching, mob violence, violation of free speech, act of discrimination, is used by our opponents in the cold war as effectively or more effectively than another bomb in a hot war.

Yes, in a world in which Jacksonville is so close and influential to Pakistan, we must be aware of the meaning and purpose of our own system. We must give a little more thought to the care and feeding of democracy. And that means more participation to make it work, all 155,000 parts of it.

Your formal training is largely over. I am sure that you are now well aware that we are dedicated to the principle that all men have a fundamental dignity, that each has the ability to develop into a better human being. You know that the gains of science and industry are the gains of all, to be shared by all as well as possible, as equitably as possible, and as soon as possible. And you know this can be done within our own system of democratic, capitalistic society. You know that the basic decisions on questions of social direction and policy are made by popular decision. And we all recognize that social change can be accomplished by consent rather than violence.

But to survive in this modern, machine-age world, we also know that we must adapt ourselves to changing times. We should know, for example, that when we have a State Constitution written eighty years ago for a specific time and set of circumstances which have changed, we must have the courage and foresight to appraise it in terms of today and to alter it to meet new circumstances and conditions. You don't cultivate any more with a wooden plow, but that's just about the way we're trying to govern Illinois. Democracy is a restless, dynamic, animate ideal. It's not static like a beautiful cathedral. To survive, our methods must keep pace with our society; we must meet new conditions with new techniques, based on our constant, changeless concepts and ideals.

I am sure you have long since learned the means of achieving these democratic objectives. You know that we are continually striving to extend, develop, and perfect our freedoms—of speech, press, religion and association—and our basic civil rights. You know that the right to vote and to select a representative and responsible government is a part of this democratic process. And most of us today realize that an intelligent, informed, interested citizenry which develops and expresses our "public opinion" is also part of this process.

Some have said it more simply, and probably more effectively than E. B. White did in 1943, in a quaint piece in the *New Yorker*, during the war:

> We received a letter from the War Writer's Board the other day asking for a statement on "The Meaning of Democracy." It presumably is our duty to comply with such a request, and it is certainly our pleasure.
>
> Surely the Board knows what democracy is. It is the line that forms on the right. It is the don't in don't shove. It is the hole in the stuffed shirt through which the sawdust trickles; it is the dent in the high hat. Democracy is the recurrent suspicion that more than half the people are right more than half of the time. It is the feeling of privacy in the voting booths, the feeling of communion in the libraries, the feeling of vitality everywhere. Democracy is a letter to the editor. Democracy is the score at the beginning of the ninth. It is an idea which hasn't been disproved yet, a song the words of which have not gone bad. It's the mustard on the hot dog and

the cream in the rationed coffee. Democracy is a request from a War Board, in the middle of the morning in the middle of a war, wanting to know what democracy is.

Why then do I say all these obvious things? You'll begin to think that to me democracy is a long, tiresome speech on a hot June day by a harassed governor to an impatient graduating class! Well, perhaps you are right. And I confess it *does* mean to me that I would like to establish some goals, some objectives toward which we can reach in the hope that working together we can continually expand and develop our cherished dream. It means simply that I urge you to put into practice the teachings that you have absorbed in your formal education. Democracy means that you are now taking your places in the running tide of a great idea, in a great, exciting period of history.

And to the governor of Illinois coming to the home town of distinguished predecessors like the two Richard Yates and Joseph Duncan, and the commencement of one of the oldest educational institutions in this state, democracy has an added special meaning: to provide full educational opportunities for as many of our citizens as possible. We can take heart as we think back to the day in 1835 when we had no common school system in Illinois; when a suspicious state legislature even seemed on the verge of refusing charters to the first three colleges in the State, on the day when a young State Legislator named Lincoln was fighting for your right to exist as a college. History records that one opponent to the bill to charter the first three Illinois schools said he was "born in a briar thicket, rocked in a hog trough and never had his genius cramped by the pestilential air of a college."

We have come a long way since then, but we have a long future and a long way to go. And it seems only right that here today I affirm my solemn task as Governor of Illinois to do everything within my power to enlarge and expand the educational facilities of our State in every way possible. In a free society there is no substitute for a conscientious and responsible citizenry. I am recommending a 70 per cent increase in State aid to common schools of Illinois, and a 22 per cent increase in funds for the State University and our Teachers Colleges. I want more people in Illinois to have the opportunities you have had. Our obligations, our responsibilities, our opportunities demand of us that we make the most of the vast reservoir of knowledge and understanding we have painstakingly gathered together in this country.

Unfortunately, too often what we study and learn about governments and systems of ordering the affairs of men rapidly fades away in the daily struggle for existence. It is easy to take our way of life for granted, and the three R's of our school days often are displaced in later days by the three N's of political life—non-voting, non-interest and non-participation. How many times have you heard the "politician" damned on the one hand for not providing Boomtown with a new artificial lake and on the other hand for spending too much money? How many of you have heard the familiar chant that all public officials are "bums"? How many of you have heard some of your older friends say, "Well, it isn't any use voting, it will be the same no matter what you do." These attitudes are a far greater threat to our way of life than the policies of the gentlemen in the Kremlin. And just remember that your public servants serve you right. I beg of you to beware of the corruption of your conscience and the ideals you have today—to beware of the subtle, corrupting effect of the apathy and cynicism you will find all about you.

Do you remember that in last year's Presidential election only about half of those who could vote did so? Do you remember that in the Congressional elections of 1946 fewer than 35 per cent of the eligible voters even bothered to express their opinion on grave national policies. Find out how many of the eligible voters participated in the elections in your own home town or county. You'll be shocked by the indifference to a thing as hard won, as precious and as costly as popular government.

If non-voting is the first of the political N's it stems in great part from the second, non-interest in our political institutions. To you this should be especially important. You have received a fine education. You have gathered a wide range of facts, figures, ideas and disciplines to help you select a course of action or make a decision. I have already noted how important to your daily life your government will be. What each of those 155,000 governing bodies in the country does will affect you. You can and will be the thinking consciences of your various communities. Because of your education you can be key people in those communities.

You will be unable to beg ignorance. You will bear more than the average responsibility not only among your own friends, but in the entire community as well. The privileges and sinecures of democratic life are not obtained for nothing. As trained and educated citizens you have a double responsibility to share in making democracy work. You can't afford to be disinterested in your school board, your conservation district, your city government, your county government, your state government, or your national government. Upon your interest rests much of the hope for the future—not just your future, but the future of everyone everywhere. Democractic apathy and economic selfishness are the assumptions on which the policy of the gentlemen in the Kremlin rest, and on which the ghosts who stalk the Reichstag rested.

The third of the political N's, non-participation, is one of the greatest challenges of our free democratic society. Now I don't mean to tell each one of you that you should run for office—God forbid! Nor is it necessary that all of you enlist for government service, although I think I could make a good case for the proposition that every man who enjoys a good education, who has profited from the advantages of our system, owes that system a couple of years of his full, uncompensated time at the local, state or national level. But I do say that through the interest of all of you, government service and public office must be made attractive to the trained and conscientious citizen. To be sure, many fine persons are found today in public service. We have men like your own graduates, Oscar Hewitt, distinguished Commissioner of Public Works in the city of Chicago, and Hugh Green, formerly speaker of the Illinois House of Representatives, who have long made significant contributions to our government. And of course I could mention some other Illinois College men who left indelible imprints on our history—William Jennings Bryan and the two Governors Yates. But the point I'm making is that government, in all the 155,000 units, is by no means as good as it could be. It's not even good enough.

I think a part of my job, and a part of the job of anyone who is in a responsible public station is to make service for the State of Illinois sufficiently attractive to lure honest, able people into public service. To this end I have made a number of specific requests of the state legislature. I have asked that the salaries of state employees be increased, and I've cut operating costs sharply to do it with the least possible additional cost to the taxpayer. I am asking that my top Department heads be given salaries commensurate with their abilities. Can you imagine, for example, the head of a business which disburses hundreds of millions being paid a salary of $8,000 a year? But we do just that in Illinois. I have asked that the State Police be taken out of politics and put on a merit basis. I have asked the legislature to strengthen the civil service system of the state to make career service more attractive. We are studying the organization of the executive department of the state to make changes which will simiplify our operations, make them more understandable, and place responsibility where it belongs.

But haphazard improvements here and there are not enough. You too have a responsibility to acquaint yourselves with the political life of your community, to interest yourselves in the selection of candidates and the operation of the elective machinery. To be a responsible citizen you can't just criticize. You and you and you are the persons who make up political parties. You must participate in political activity. It's your government, and you must help if you want to keep it that way.

These are some of the political facts of life you will soon be facing as you go out to make your own contributions to our free society. Our way of doing things is being challenged all over the world, from the beautiful boulevards of Paris to the packed plains of China. All the fine words and platitudes, mine included, won't win this war of two basically different ways of life. But what happens in those 155,000 governments—in Jacksonville, in Springfield, or in Washington—can and will have much to do with the outcome of the twentieth century struggle between freedom and tyranny. To you we turn in hope.

SOLDIERS AND SAILORS REUNION, SALEM
July 28

I didn't come back to Salem to your famous Soldiers and Sailors Reunion today to talk about politics and the affairs of the State of Illinois. Much as I would like to tell you about what happened in Springfield in the past six months and what was accomplished and what wasn't accomplished. I am going to spare you. Because I am here today to pay official respects to this great tradition, this Reunion which springs from the mortal anguish of our Civil War to preserve the Union of the States, and to pay my official and personal respects to your distinguished guest of honor, Admiral William H. P. Blandy of the United States Navy, who has dedicated his life and his remarkable talents to the preservation of this Union of the States in the time allotted to us to live on this earth.

I am glad he has seen fit to come to Illinois and I am glad he came here to Salem to the Soldiers and Sailors Reunion, although you no longer reunite as soldiers and sailors in the two World Wars which have already made of our generation the bloodiest interval in the Christian era. We had best not forget those wars and what they cost in blood, treasure and disorder, as we had best not forget the origin of this reunion, the Civil War, and the ghastly cost of disunion and a divided people.

I don't think there is much basic division between us. I think we've learned a lot about the pride of self-preservation, about what we are as a people and what we want as a people. It doesn't make much difference what we are—farmer, worker, housewife, businessman, Republican, Democrat—we all want about the same things: peace and prosperity. Not peace or prosperity, but peace and prosperity. It's both or neither, because without enduring peace there can be no enduring prosperity. Conversely there can be no enduring peace without a healthy, strong, productive United States, on which the equilibrium of the whole world depends.

When you come right down to it, that's what we want, all of us. And where we disagree is how to get it. Some people say we should not aid the economic recovery of other countries. Some people think we can remain peaceful and prosperous while the rest of the world is hungry and envious. Some even think we can go on selling without buying. And I suspect the large question mark of the future is whether we have learned that insurance is cheaper than disaster—whether we have learned that it is better to insure against wars than to pay for them. The insurance, economic and military, is expensive, and in the past democracies have usually preferred to save the insurance premiums and pay for the wars. It seems to me that the history of democracy is the history of the sacrifice of foreign policy to domestic expediency. England , for example, did not want conscription because it interfered with personal freedom and took men out of productive employment. But England paid an almost mortal price for the war she didn't want and was not prepared to fight.

But, however uncertain we still are on the economic cost of peace, however uncertain we are as to the fine line between strengthening others and weakening ourselves, we see much less division on the necessity of military strength in this period of convulsive readjustment in the world.

AMERICAN LEGION STATE CONVENTION, CHICAGO
August 5

TO BE QUITE HONEST I am grateful for this opportunity to pay my respects as Governor to the Department of Illinois. I have been a member of the American Legion for many years and I am proud that the Bloomington Post is named for my first cousin who died in World War I. But this is the first time I've ever been invited to the platform. I had begun to think that being Governor of Illinois had no redeeming features, but I feel better about it today, thanks to your courtesies and the honor you do my office.

I think Illinois is recognizing its obligation to the veteran. In my opinion, emphasis now and in the future must be on assistance to veterans who actually need economic aid, special training and medical services. And I think, too, that it is in the self interest of the veterans' organizations to see to it that there is no preventable abuse of the generosity of the people in meeting their obligation to the veteran; to see to it that aid to veterans does not come to be regarded in the public mind as a "gravy train".

I think the people of Illinois and America will always be generous when it comes to financing legitimate recognition of its creditors —the veteran. But they will rebel against unreasonble demands just as they will rebel against payroll padding, waste, extravagance, or any form of inefficient administration of public funds. And when I approved a cut recommended by the Budgetary Commission in the appropriation for the Illinois Veterans Commission, I did so because I felt that its services could and must be rendered to the veteran at less cost to the taxpayer. I will continue to effect such savings to the taxpayer however, whenever and wherever I can throughout the state administration. And I am confident, in spite of the doubts expressed by some, that the Veterans Commission can and will discharge its mission of service to the veteran during the next two years adequately and efficiently, and well within the appropriation of two milion dollars.

After all, the veteran is a taxpayer, too, and he's a citizen first and a veteran second. I think I spent as much time in and around this last war as most of the people in this room and, unless I'm very much mistaken the average veteran looks upon himself first of all as an American citizen, and not as a member of a special class. He is proud of the service that he gave his country and conscious of the meaning of that sacrifice. Yet he neither demands nor expects any unreasonable reward or special privileges at the hands of his fellow citizens. But he does demand, like his fellow citizens, that the government and the free society he sacrificed to save shall endure and afford him the blessings of American life—a job, a home and the advantages of American citizenship for his children.

And I conceive it to be my duty as a public offical and as a legionnaire along with you to do what I can, not only to never let the people forget what he as a veteran did, but to give him what he as a citizen expects of a government in the best of our tradition. And I know that's what you expect of all your public officials and of one another as legionnaires.

We all know that the nation looks for leadership to the men and women who have fought to defend this nation in time of war. An impressive representation of that leadership has come from the American Legion through the years. That is a record in which all of us here take pride. I know it is a record which every legionnaire wants to preserve and enhance.

May your convention of 1949, through constructive thought and action, yield still further evidence of the idealism and high purpose to which the American Legion is dedicated and of which the veterans like all our citizens are beneficiaries.

LITCHFIELD CHAMBER OF COMMERCE
September 27

I DON'T FEEL MUCH like a politician tonight and not at all like the Governor. So I hope you will not be disappointed if I am quite informal in my remarks, and if I don't attempt to be profound about taxes, the Cold War, the high cost of living, or any of the other weighty issues of the day. Not that I don't have some opinions on those questions, but I have no reason to think they are more competent than your own. And furthermore, I thought you might prefer that I chat with you on a more personal, intimate basis—that you would be interested in hearing about some of the experiences I have had and the impressions I have gained about the governorship of Illinois since I took office last January. After all, we are virtually next door neighbors and there's nothing wrong with neighbors chatting over the back fence for a few minutes!

You know, before I somewhat unexpectedly became a politician I used to be just a simple barefoot LaSalle Street lawyer, a farmer, and a sort of intermittent—itinerant—government servant and diplomat. I used to lecture occasionally at universities and before audiences around the country on foreign affairs. They even paid me fees to talk—which is another reason politics is not as attractive as it should be. It was a cinch. In those days after the war all you had to do was to talk darkly about the atomic bomb, bacteriological extermination, the decline and fall of the British Empire, damn the sinister Russians, beat your breast self-righteously about the United States and wind up with a fervent prayer for the United Nations, and a five or six point program; five or six points depending on whether you thought you could get away with a demand for tax reduction, economy and more free enterprise, coupled with emphatic insistence on an impregnable national defense in the atomic age and a plea for America financing a world crusade to stop Communism. It may sound hard to you, but it's a cinch; you can't miss! The audience approves of everything you say! They're spellbound. When you've finished they thank you nervously and earnestly for your message—what a word!—and wander into the night with their apprehensions confirmed, their confusion enlarged and their perspective diminished. Well, that's all changed now—my horizons are the State of Illinois.

When I decided to run for Governor last year I did so with my eyes wide open; I knew it was a job involving many problems and many responsibilities. It didn't take me long to find out I wasn't wrong—I had merely underestimated. I found that the problems that are laid on the Governor's doorstep from day to day are of infinitely greater variety than the average citizen realizes. It is an office in which there has been a tremendous growth of responsibility in the last two decades or so. It is one of those jobs in which there are no hours and no holidays; in which you literally work day and night, and pause every once in a while to wonder if you are really getting any place in accomplishing the things you are trying to do.

In one respect, at least, it reminds me of international conferences and something I wrote in London in a weary moment:

I live in a sea of words
Where the nouns and the adjectives flow;
Where the verbs speak of actions
That never take place
And the sentences come and go.

I found too that in many respects the governorship is a paradox. Because it is the highest elective office in the state people are inclined to think that the Governor can do anything or everything. Actually, the Governor's authority is very definitely limited by the Constitution and by our statutes. But a great many people seem to have the idea that all I have to do is snap my fingers and magical things will happen; that a bridge will be built, a new highway will go in, or even that I can get your federal income taxes or your rent reduced—or that an airport will appear. I am happy to say, by the way, that we hope to be of some help to your Litchfield airport.

Frankly, I have been surprised and a little startled by the faith which many people who are not very familiar with the processes of our government, have in the power of the Governor. Some of the appeals that are made to me through the mails are amazing. Just this week a woman wrote me a letter suggesting I compel her ex-husband to pay her $1,200 back alimony. A man wrote to ask whether I thought it was true that Sam Houston once shot an Indian at five thousand yards, and shooting over a hill at that! Various people who write songs send their efforts to me for judgment and endorsement, even though I can't carry a tune. And I was cautioned at an early age to diminish my volume in church.

A mysterious note came to my desk the other day. It was very brief. "Look into license number so and so, 1948 Black Ford sedan." The note was signed "Conscientious Objector." A farm wife wrote demanding that I do something to keep her neighbor's cattle, whose pedigree she judged to be much lower than that of her own herd, from mingling with her livestock and thus endangering the breed. Even the young credit me with vast powers. A fifth grade farm boy wrote to ask whether he could be compelled to "walk farther than my mailbox" to catch the school bus. I suspect he was looking to me for an excuse to get out of going to school. Having ridden a bicycle four or five blocks myself I couldn't write him an exemplary letter about how I trudged three miles through snow and ice morning and evening to win a little education.

Dozens of other examples could be cited, but that gives you an idea. About five hundred people write to me every day on the average. At times, as during legislative sessions, when people were making known their views on pending bills, the volume of correspondence was much greater.

A considerable part of a Governor's mail consists of invitations to attend various public functions. If I were twins I couldn't accept one-tenth of these invitations and get any work done. In fact, I cannot accept as many as I would like to, and still do justice to my responsibilities to the state government, which is the biggest business in the state. Invitations of one kind or another for public appearances average eight or ten daily, and I am not sure whether I should be flattered or whether it's merely a case of people being curious to see what I look like.

But I do like my job, and I am grateful to those of you in Litchfield and Montgomery County who helped put me in office. At the same time I think I understand why defeated candidates always congratulate victors. I not only like my job, I want more than I have ever wanted anything to improve the quality of public administration in Illinois. I want the State of Illinois to have a state government recognized everywhere as progressive, competent and enlightened as the people of our state are recognized everywhere to be. I not only want it—but we must have it. With the apalling cost of government, people won't tolerate inefficiency much longer.

The population of our state has grown by over two million people in the last twenty years. In the same way, the demands upon government have grown. This is true with the state government as well as the Federal government, and doubtless Mayor Peterson would tell you it is true of local government. As the activities of state government have increased, so have the administrative tasks grown more complex and demanding. I am amused by stories I have heard about the way of life of governors of Illinois in an earlier day, how they had plenty of leisure time for hunting and fishing trips and the like, not to mention poker and story-telling sessions. If they were to step back into the job today, I am pretty sure they wouldn't recognize it. And I'm pretty sure they wouldn't like it either.

It was in the '30s, during the administration of the late Governor Horner, that the demands upon State government for new services had their greatest growth. The widespread unemployment of the depression days, and the evolution of social security, placed tremendous new responsibilities upon the state. Since then the emergencies precipitated by the war period and the post-war reorganization era have added still others. More and more people have come to look to the state to help them meet their needs for better schools, better health services, better roads and streets, for hospitals and airports and better care for the aged and the needy.

A review of the new activities which have been undertaken by state government in the last twenty years is quite revealing: old age pensions, aid to dependent children, unemployment compensation, state aid for county health departments, housing and slum clearance, the workmen's compensation and occupational diseases act and a dozen other laws for the benefit of workers; the liquor control law, the motor vehicle anti-theft and compulsory insurance laws, delinquency prevention, state support for airport building and tuberculosis sanitariums, oil and gas conservation, the liquor control act and the veterans' bonus and assistance acts. A complete list of new enactments involving new state responsibilities in that period would be five or six times that length, but that is indicative of the way in which state services have been broadened.

This trend toward increased reliance upon government is quite logical. In part it is a result of our increasing knowledge, and our desire to put that knowledge to the uses of other people. In part it is in recognition of the obvious fact that individuals and private groups cannot possibly do all the things that must be done for their own protection and advancement, whether it be safeguarding their insurance investments, seeing that they pay a fair price for their public utility services, or providing a system of insurance for the unemployed. In part this trend toward expanding government is a consequence of social change, of a changing public concept as to the duties of government. No single reason offers a complete explanation of increasing governmental activity; it is an inevitable outgrowth of modern civilization.

In the case of our state government, a great deal of the expansion which has taken place has been in activities which formerly were looked upon as obligations of local government. In other words, the state has assumed a portion of the expense of local government in a number of important fields—particularly support of the schools, in public health, in the care of those requiring relief and pensions, and in such forms of aid as street maintenance through sharing of the gasoline tax, aid to hospital construction, recreational lakes, etc. etc.

Let me illustrate what this has meant in terms of the dollar you pay in state taxes. An analysis of the appropriations made by the legislature this year, shows that just a little over seven cents of each state tax dollar goes for the executive, legislative and judicial branches of government, the basic operating arms of state government. The bulk of the tax dollar goes for specific purposes largely in the category of "distributive" grants to local government.

For example, twenty-two and a fraction cents of our state dollar goes for education, including the 140 millions which will be distributed to the public schools during the current two-year fiscal period. Twenty years ago that appropriation for schools was sixteen millions, which indicates how ideas as to the state's responsibility to the schools have changed. Thirty-four cents of our state dollar goes for welfare purposes, including 307,000 people who are on our pension and public assistance rolls and the more than 47,000 wards in the state welfare institutions. Twenty-one and a half cents of each state dollar goes for highways, and as you know, the state receives only the revenue from one cent of the three-cent state gasoline tax. One cent goes to the counties and one cent to the cities.

Look at it another way.When the state government of Illinois was reorganized in 1917 during the Lowden administration, there were established nine code departments to administer the various functions of state government. Today we have thirteen departments and a half dozen permanent, major commissions performing specific administrative functions, and scores with less important or temporary functions. I am not saying we have an ideal administrative arrangement by any means, because we do not, but I am saying the creation of those new departments and commissions indicates again the extent to which the activities of the state government have broadened.

I hope the fact that I was invited here indicates you do have an active interest in the affairs of state government, and that this interest is typical of all the people of Illinois. Certainly the better informed our people are about their government, the greater the interest they take in its affairs, the better our government is going to be.

The evidence of greater public interest in government is a healthy sign. I for one am optimistic about the future of our democratic institutions and our ability to deal with new problems as they arise. I am well aware that there are many who say we have too much government, and who see something sinister in every effort of government to cope with new developments in new ways. And I am equally familiar with those who complain bitterly and incessantly about tax increases and the dreadful cost of government who are often the first to demand more state services.

Government cannot remain static, anymore than society can. It cannot remain static because government itself is both a phase of life and a social institution. It cannot be separated from life, or from the influences that are everywhere bringing changes in established modes of thought and action. If it were to try to stand apart from these influences it would lose its force and meaning; it would fail to perform one of the chief functions for which it is established. The trend toward passing on the responsibility and burden from city to state to nation is familiar to us all. It is dangerous. Is it inevitable? I suggest that the only way it can be controlled is to stand ready to furnish locally the services people demand.

The first Roosevelt—Teddy Roosevelt—had a reassuring word about the transformation of government which he recognized as taking place in his day. He pointed out that government had taken the place of individual action in a hundred ways, as in fire protection, drainage, water, light and transportation services, and he observed: "It would be an absurdity to expect every man to look after his own interests in all these matters, or to say he had lost the power of individual initiative because he delegated any or all of them to the province of public officers."

I hope we will never be timid in our approach to new problems, that we will always face the future with confidence and courage, and that we will leave to our children a heritage even brighter and richer than that which was handed down to us. Most of all, I hope you and people like you all over Illinois are awakening to the tremendous importance—measured either in cost or services—of the state government. We have been too prone to expend most of our interest and study on the national government. But local and state governments are important too, and getting more and more so. Also, partisanship and party division on issues become less and less important at the state and local level. I don't care so much, for example, whether you agree or disagree with me on any specific state problem. But I do care if people are not interested enough in their business to have an intelligent understanding and view of the problem.

JUVENILE DELINQUENCY PREVENTION CONFERENCE, CHICAGO
November 4

THE SOCIAL PROBLEMS THAT confront us in this era of post-war readjustment are many. But none is graver, none more impelling than that of juvenile delinquency and youth in crime.

Throughout America, in large cities and small, we see the tragic picture of juveniles and teen-agers before the courts, charged not merely with delinquency, but with the most heinous offenses in the catalog of crime —murder, manslaughter, rape and armed robbery.

It is a distressing, disquieting fact that the average age of criminals convicted of the most serious crimes has fallen into the teen-age brackets. There has been an alarming increase in crimes committed by offenders between the ages of twelve and nineteen. This tragic phenomenon is widespread; it is not confined to any particular area of the country. It is prevalent in all sections and especially in the large centers of population.

A sorrowful figure is the youthful offender at the bar of justice, charged with a serious violation of a criminal law. No one would waste sympathy on the hard, calloused adult professional criminal who knows the consequences of crime. But a different reaction occurs to the pitiful figure of the youthful violator, to the tragic scene of boys and girls who come through the courts every day to be started on the way to penal servitude. Auto thieves, gunmen, burglars, felons, murderers—before they are old enough to vote—an appalling figure to contemplate.

We might wish that we could blot out such a picture, that we could escape the impact of it, and see only the happy and wholesome side of young America. But it would gain us nothing to attempt to evade reality, and try to overlook this alarming phase of our total crime problem.

I think the realization is growing among our people that we are paying too much for the apprehension and conviction of criminals, and too little for the prevention of crime. That is a healthy sign, because clearly the only antidote for juvenile crime is intelligent dealing with the factors that create criminal tendencies.

I wonder how many have stopped to consider the cost of crime in America. Its cost is staggering. Crime is a big business, by whatever yardstick you measure it. It runs to some twenty-five billions of dollars each year, when you include the cost of our penitentiaries, jails, and reformatories; the cost of maintaining police forces and the courts and the loss and destruction of property. That figure represents an average of $170 a year for every man, woman and child in the United States.

But that is not the only cost of crime, or even the heaviest cost. The greatest cost of all is in human values, in the wreckage of lives, in innocent victims, in the blighted future of boys and girls, and in broken families.

All of us know that our crime record here in Chicago is nothing to brag about, and it is small satisfaction to tell ourselves that it is no worse than that of some other cities. We have had too many juvenile crimes here, of very recent memory, to be unaware that this is *not* somebody else's problem, but our very own.

I do not pose as an expert in sociology, and I doubt that I shall be able to suggest any approach to this problem that you haven't heard before. But I can emphasize some truths which, if universally recognized and applied by our young people and their elders, would in time reflect themselves in a reduced crime rate.

No particular person or group, no single influence in the community can prevent juvenile crime or be held accountable for its current upsurge. We all recognize, I believe, that the first responsibility of the proper training of children rests with parents. If any doubt that, they have only to consider that 79% of the prisoners in the state prison at Stateville, which is typical, come from homes where there was indifferent or inadequate parental care, or abnormal conditions of living.But parents cannot do all of the job; part of it must be done by the schools, the churches and the organizations which deal with young people. Part of it must be done by those who produce our movies, our newspapers, our radio and television programs and those who draw our comics. Part of it too must be done by government through intelligent administration of the welfare services, competent enforcement of the laws, and the elimination of those conditions in the community which are contributory to crime.

And somehow we must impress upon the boys and girls in the high schools, and even in the elementary grades, that part of the responsibility rests with them. We must do a better job than we have done of making our young people realize that their happiness and welfare rests pretty much in their own hands. When we tell today's children they will be tomorrow's leaders, we must try to give meaning to the phrase, to make them see that the kind of city, the kind of nation they will live in in their adult lives will be of their own making.

But I always hesitate when I find myself attempting to give advice to young people. I asked one young man not long ago what his main problem in life was and he replied: "Old fogies." I straightened my shoulders, tried to look a little younger and speculated whether he was referring to me. Old fogies are a problem. They have been in every generation. It is hard for some people to grow old without becoming cynical, but I would say to young people:listen to the old and young courteously but be careful who influences you. If you run across those who see no good in the world, who say that everything is going to the dogs and that most people are rascals, don't believe them.But don't reject wisdom from whatever source it may come. Some of your elders have lived a long time, some of them have learned much. The trick is to select the truly wise ones and listen to them.

I would hazard one other bit of advice. Don't let anyone convince you it is clever to violate the laws, even in minor ways, because others may have done so or because you think you may be able to get away with it. Experience proves you won't get away with it, at least for long. Consider this: At the state prison at Pontiac the average age of inmates is nineteen. All our state prisons are heavily populated with prisoners in their early twenties. Just a few years ago they were in high school like you. They were the ones who thought they could "get away with it." In hundreds of cases their lives of crime began with malicious mischief and small misdemeanors and grew into something worse. How much better it is to emulate those who have won places of leadership in the activities of your school, whether it be making touchdowns, making good music in the band, or making good grades in the classroom!

Everyone cannot be acclaimed as a leader, of course, but everyone can find a useful place whether it be in school life or adult life. Every high school student can make a contribution to his school and his community, and it isn't necessary that he be endowed with any special talents. Let me cite an example of what I mean: young people can perhaps do more than any other group to win the continuing battle against intolerance and prejudice. This battle will in time be won. It will be won by young people with ideals and new vision, just as the ideals, the vision and the energies of the young have carried succeeding generations of Americans forward to constantly higher social standards and achievements.

In some respects our present high school students are a unique group. They grew up in a nation at war, under conditions that were highly abnormal. Many, indeed most of them, have had their lives affected in one way or another by these unusual wartime conditions. In many cases mothers as well as fathers were in uniform or in the factories; older sisters and brothers were away from home; normal family relationships were disrupted. Thousands of children were thrown on their own resources to an extent not normal in ordinary times.

No doubt this situation has been responsible in part for a lack of adult direction which we know has caused some young boys and girls to fall into criminal ways. But by the same token it has placed a greater responsibility on the shoulders of you high school students of today. It has made you a bit more mature, a bit more self-reliant, and I hope a better judge of life's real values than some of us of earlier generations.

It is a safe assertion that most of you who are in high school today have a greater perception, a wider perspective, a better grasp of human affairs than did most of us in my prep school days.

Not long ago I ran across a sonnet written by an American youth flying with the Royal Canadian Air Force. The young man's name was John Gillespie Magee, Jr., and he was killed in combat in December of 1942, just shortly after he had written his sonnet, which he called "High Flight". He was just nineteen years old, one year out of high school. Archibald MacLeish thought enough of "High Flight" to place it on exhibition in the Library of Congress in Washington. It reads:

Oh I have climbed the surly bounds of earth
And danced the skies on laughter-silvered wings
Sunward I've climbed and joined the tumbling mirth
Of sun-split clouds—and done a hundred things
You have not dreamed of—wheeled and soared and swung
High in the sunlit
Silence, hov'ring there I've chased the shouting
wind along and flung
My eager craft through footless halls of air
Up, up the long, delirious, burning blue
I've topped the wind swept heights with easy grace
Where never lark, or even eagle flew
And, while with silent lifting mind I've trod
The high, untrespassed sanctity of space,
Put out my hand and touched the face of God.

There is no ceiling on how high any of you can go in this America in which you are privileged to live. That is why those of us who are older look upon it as such a tragedy when young people neglect to take advantage of their opportunities, when they fail to recognize the rich rewards that await those who have the will to gain them.

That is why I say to you: hold fast to your dreams, your hopes, your high ideals. They are the greatest assets of youth, and youth is truly the hope of America and all the world.

DECATUR ASSOCIATION OF COMMERCE
November 30

I T IS QUITE APPARENT that it wasn't curiosity about the new Governor and the care and feeding of political infants, or accidents, that induced you to induce me to come to Decatur tonight with your fellow townsman and my esteemed Director of Agriculture, Roy Yung. Rather it was to permit me as Governor to join you in honoring Henry Bolz, who has been an outstanding Secretary of an outstanding Association of Commerce for a long time, and the past presidents and directors of the Decatur Association of Commerce.

I read here that Mr. La Forgee has said: "The finest thing I can say: I have lived in Decatur and I have had a part in it." I like that. In fact, I can't see how it could be improved in brevity, sincerity or emphasis—unless, of course, you were to substitute Bloomington, my home town!

If Decatur, Illinois, is the best, or certainly one of the best cities in which to live and work in the United States, it is not an accident. It is due in large measure to community effort and enterprise which is useless without leadership. And that is why this Association of Commerce exists which has harnessed, organized and directed community leadership here so long and so well. Thirty or thirty-five years ago Decatur's industrial growth was limited by its water supply. So you built Lake Decatur. I believe this was one of the first cities in the country to vote taxes on itself to improve its schools and raise the salaries of its teachers. You have faced the necessity for improving and expanding your hospital facilities and you are doing something about it.

You even provided a home for a great and colorful Illinois figure—Richard Oglesby—although I'm not sure that the Association of Commerce had much to do with that!

But there is no doubt that this very active and enlightened Association does not let Decatur forget that the building of a community is never finished. I'm sure that here in Decatur you are never permitted to forget that there is a limitless need for citizens in business, in labor, in the professions, in agriculture, who are willing to sacrifice enough of their time and complacency—who are willing, if you please, to pay in full their debt to a free society—to do the everlasting job of community betterment through this Association, through the churches, the labor unions, the service clubs and all the other group means of expressing disinterested citizenship. All of these groups have more to do than they can do. All of them provide the means for service and leadership. All of them need men who are willing to give of their time and leisure. Perhaps most important of all, they provide an opportunity for self education about government, which is the biggest, most expensive, most essential and most intricate business in which we are all engaged. That this city has become a major industrial, educational, business and residential ornament of Illinois is due less, I daresay, to the blessings of a fortunate geographical situation than to good citizen leadership. And I hope and pray that more and more of the good, responsible people here and elsewhere will find more and more time and inclination for public service, for service on boards and committees and to do the thousand and one chores that make a community prosper; that root out the twin evils of apathy and cynicism which nourish corruption, carelessness and bad government.

What any administration can accomplish depends in season and out far more on public attitudes and understanding than people sometimes realize. Too often you people who are not in politics in the active, combatant sense feel as I did once that "the politicians" and the legislature are insensitive and remote and there is little you can do but vote on election day. But that sense of frustration, futility and bewilderment dries up, it seems to me, vigilant and positive public expression which is the greatest force of all. Then, too, as Bryce said long ago, excessive partisanship is one of the great hazards of democracy and a two party system. Too many of us think in grooves of prejudice: if it's a Republican administration it's reactionary and corrupt; if it is a Democratic administration it is wasteful and, of course, corrupt too. What ordinary people don't always realize is that I or anyone in my position have to fight inertia, tradition, corruption, political avarice and implacable partisanship. They are all enemies of good or at least better government, and you either fight them all the time or you surrender to them. Surrender is the easy thing to do and you can get away with it for a shamefully long time. The point is that if the people, the non-political laymen, are with you, positively and actively with you, the fight is easier and you'll win it because they are stronger than all the self interested groups and traditions combined, and no one knows it better than a politician. But if public opinion is silent, if the people are indifferent or inanimate, then you have to cajole and plead, give, surrender and compromise to get much of anything done, and pretty soon you're licked, and then of course you lose what public support you had to boot!

I could and would like to talk at length about the posture of our affairs nationally and internationally and what seems to me the importance from either point of view—not to mention our pocket books—of a more active and conscious public concern for government at all its levels. I don't mean just the great national issues in Washington that preoccupy the bulk of our time and thought, but what goes on in Springfield and in your City Hall and why. After all, some 155,000 units of government have sprung up under the spreading arms of our federal system. From the long view government is not going to be much better or much worse than its component parts, and its largest component parts are the states. And Illinois is one of the largest of these. Finally, we can't afford bad government financially and we can't afford it morally or tactically in a world and an age that is watching us shrewdly, hopefully, perhaps a little cynically.

But I'll have to save all that for another time. Moreover, you know it anyway. What I do want to say before I subside and end these banalities is inspired by a request I had the other day from a fellow townsman of yours. He seemed to have some doubt as to whether I was really a Democrat. I've run into similar confusion and not a little criticism from Democrats as well as Republicans since I abandoned a prosperous, peaceful life and became a politician. I'm not sure, frankly, what kind of Democrat I am. But I am sure what kind of Democrat I am not. As I said to the Herald-Tribune Forum in New York last month, "I am not one of those who believes we should have a Democratic regime because it is good for the Democratic party. If the Democratic party is not good for Illinois and the nation, it is not good for me, or for Democrats!"

I do not claim to have fixed principles by which every issue is to be automatically resolved. I do not think that government has to be big in order to be good, I think it should be as small in scope and as local in character as possible. But I also think that the job which needs doing must shape and delimit the area of governmental activity. And I think any necessary task that can be done best by government should not be neglected because of any unyielding notions about the proper size and extent of government.

As Governor of Illinois I cannot shape any national or international policies. But I can improve the probity, the efficiency and the morality of state government—or break my heart and head in the attempt. I can influence our policies in education, welfare, taxation and all of the hundred and one housekeeping jobs that are within my province.

If something needs doing that costs more money I can ask for it, as I have. If something costs more money than it is worth I can oppose it, as I have. If our old Constitution makes for waste, law evasion and injustice, I can say so regardless of the opposition, and I have done that too. Moreover, I think the best government is the best politics— for Democrats and Republicans alike.

I suppose it should be added that I am an "international-ist." I believe that peace is the most important unfinished business of our generation; that we are going to be in this brutal, costly cold war for a long time to come and that we had better win it if we want to preserve the Western idea of individualism and freedom which has been in the ascendancy so long.

I don't like government doles. I don't like subsidies. I don't like any interferences with free markets, free men, and free enterprise. I like freedom to succeed or to fail. I think free-dom of opportunity is more important than any 'security' that government can promise. But I know there can be no real freedom without economic justice, social justice, equal-ity of opportunity and a fair chance for every individual to make the most of himself. And I know that there is little the man on the assembly line or the plow can do to affect the chain of events which may close his factory or foreclose his mortgage. Discontented, desperate men will sell freedom very cheap.

The basic political rift of our day in this country is by no means between those who favor individual liberty as against those who favor subjugation of the individual to the state. The rift concerns how far government is to go to attain the economic and social atmosphere in which the utmost indi-vidual liberty can thrive. Stated another way: how far government must impair some individual freedom to pre-serve more.

No one wants government to control every detail of human life. But anyone who talks of a return to the good old days when government acted only as a policeman is on his way to a museum.

The real argument is between those who want govern-ment to do more at once and those who counsel caution lest we lose more of the Jeffersonian ideal of individual supre-macy than we save. There are, of course, a lot of sideshows, posturing and windmill tilting to catch the crowd's fancy, but when the theatrical props are laid aside I can't see that the responsible 'too muchers' are all agents of selfish interest, or the 'not enoughers' agents of Moscow. The conflict is not going to be solved by epithets and slogans like 'Communist', 'Socialist', 'statism', 'welfare', 'Fair Deal', or 'New Deal.'

Somewhere in between lies the area where 'welfare' ideas and 'enterprise' ideas sometimes clash but more often merge. If we continue, as we have, with caution and thorough discussion; if we don't forget who or what we are trying to save—the American individual and his freedom—I am not worried about ruinous reaction on the one hand or radical misadventure on the other, because the American individual is a very sensible fellow.

Like the elderly optimist who attributed his happy old age to the fact that he 'just learned to cooperate with the inevitable', we can cooperate with progress for a greater, happier Illinois. And I'm optimistic that we will.

ILLINOIS RETAIL FARM EQUIPMENT ASSOCIATION, PEORIA
December 3

EVERY TIME I TALK about the state's finances I end up with a sort of hopeless feeling—the subject is so large, so complicated and so dreary that few will invest the time and effort to even try to analyze and understand the state budget. The result is that the demand for economy, which is as old and insistent as the opposition to taxes, produces little result. These habits of mind and speech, defeat or elect candidates for public office in our country frequently, but they don't improve government because they are just old refrains. Actually, an informed, positive public expression is the greatest force of all. Inertia, prejudice, and cynicism on the part of the non-political layman outside government can be as avarice or corruption on the part of politicans inside government.

I think it would be a good thing if associations such as yours would analyze the state budget like you study your own budgets. It would lead to a greater understanding of public finance and its management which means so much to every one of you since taxes represent such a substantial part of your business expense. An uneducated resentment is never effective for positive good, but understanding and a positive objective is.

Certainly I would welcome your interest in this intricate and emotional subject of budgets and taxes because I know that regardless of our political affiliations, regardless of the fact that you are in private business and I happen to be in politics at the moment, we both want the same things for Illinois.

Besides, I need a lot of help if I am going to accomplish much of what you hired me to do. And you can't help very much unless you understand the problem, the whole problem, not just the fraction or portion of it that appears to most affect you, because it all affects us, and it affects us all. Government is the biggest business there is. You are all in it whether you like it nor not, and its hand is in your pocket day and night. How anyone with a grade school education can any longer be indifferent to government from a purely self-interested, material point of view is beyond me, let alone from any ideological and abstract consideration of principle.

In my brief political experience I've had to learn some things I just vaguely understood the hard way—by the shock method. For example, that the relation of any proposal to the public good is not a sufficient measure of its virtue. In fact, the closer that relationship is the more likely that it will arouse opposition. In politics you see it is not always good to allow an executive who does not belong to your party to accomplish much. Indeed it's dangerous. Hence, too often the old strategy is to encourage failures and minimize successes. And the old refrains and epithets are useful weapons on people who are not informed and whose prejudices can be so easily aroused.

In a country like ours where commerce and industry have developed to such an extent, the public interest in business keeps mounting constantly and governmental interference keeps increasing in the proportion that such enterprises impinge upon the public interest. Whether we like it or not, that interference is political and it is, therefore, absurd for intelligent men of affairs to say that they abhor politics and will have nothing to do with it. Every measure presented to any legislative body, every act taken by any administration—national, state or municipal—every appointment to an office, or, for that matter, to a menial public position, is a political matter.

And if politics is not held in high repute it is not because its business is unimportant or lacks inherent dignity, neither is it solely due to the politicians. The real blame is on us—if I can step out of character for a moment—who for generations have relaxed our hold on our most important business. The word "politics" has become almost a reproach. The so-called respectable shun it. They will not enter the political arena for fear of soiling the hem of their skirts. The consequence—this vast, all-important field of human action and power is not infrequently in the control of those who do not mind soiled skirts. In fact, they are offered a premium for keeping the arena befouled. In effect you say: "We shall not enter your precincts because they are foul", and the silent answer is: "Thanks for the formula by which you can be kept out, we want it to ourselves." They don't want competition or to run the risk of having control wrested from them. As a matter of self-preservation they are almost compelled to keep the arena unclean.

Our society is becoming increasingly complicated. Life itself is becoming so complex that the average individual finds far greater difficulty in adjusting himself to proper living than did our fathers and grandfathers. In a country so highly developed as ours and one whose destiny has brought her to the very top of the mountain and clothed her with responsibility and prestige which made her the leader of the democratic forces of the world, the individual, no matter how free he may be, can't possibly remain in isolation. Our interdependence is so great that mere living in an orderly society involves being in politics. Whether we like it or not, the forces which operate all around us, whose impacts we feel in our daily existence, compel some form of organization in every field of endeavor. We organize in labor unions, in chambers of commerce, in agricultural associations, in mining associations, even in our philanthropies.

In business organizations, not alone wealth is acquired, but great power as well, and unless that power will be used with some sense of responsibility toward the general good, government will step in, and government is politics.

I should like to see the businessmen of this state develop and experiment with methods for the elimination of causes which tend to increase interference by government. There ought to be no need for government to seek to compel fair trade practices. There ought to be no need for government to seek to compel fair employment practices. Those who enjoy the privilege of employing others ought to regard fair practices in respect of employment as a solemn obligation. There ought to be no need for the establishment of minimum wages by law. Every employer worthy of the privilege he enjoys should feel bound to pay a living wage to everyone fit to be employed for any task. If employers concerned themselves with the health and old age of their workers, the enormous losses which our economy suffers through illness and the public expense of social security would recede. Private enterprise committed to such a program could have little to fear from the blandishments of socialism and communism.

You may conclude that I believe emphatically in what is called for want of a better word "free enterprise." I do. But free enterprise in our world must result in more than profit for the few. It must be a source of well being for the many, or it won't be free very long.

You may also have concluded that I believe in less government interference, not more. You are right again, but if business does not do the job the people will demand and they will get the interference.

Our effort should always be to make America strong in terms of small, independent local governments. They are—they will always be—an essential condition for the flourishing of a real democracy and of an unfettered and forward-looking economy. Our objective should be the steady relinquishment by higher levels of power and direction over lower, the constant pushing of governmental authority and administration back as close to the people as they can go. Government should function in as close and as continuous a relationship with the citizen as you do with your customers and your employees.

There is, however, no more magic in smallness than in bigness—in government as in business. The virtues of increased emphasis on government at the local level will not be realized unless there is responsibility. The community which would govern itself must accept responsibility for governmental functions—for law enforcement, for the supplying of necessary services, for providing the necessary finances, for the myriad other matters which have come to be recognized as the legitimate concern of government.

I don't know whether it can be done, whether people really care enough to do it. But I know that as small businessmen, as persons whose daily business lives are object lessons in the acceptance and discharge of local responsibilities, your influence, your example, your active interest, can do much to arrest the present trend and help us turn back to a pattern of full local self-government in those matters which can, and should, be handled at home. I suggest to you that, by so doing, you will be striking a mighty blow in defense of a national way of life which has owed so much to small business and in which small business has had a chance to live and prosper.

NATIONAL REORGANIZATION CONFERENCE SPONSORED BY THE CITIZENS COMMITTEE FOR THE HOOVER REPORT, WASHINGTON D.C.
December 12

Y OU MAY WONDER why I am here and whether a Governor of a big state does not have enough problems of his own without concerning himself with reorganization of the executive branch of the Federal Government. I assure you I do have. And some of them seem to arise from very strange concepts of the functions of a state executive. The other day a woman wrote asking me to do something about tile floors in restaurants. She said they hurt her feet!

Of course, the fact is that the Hoover Commission and its recommendations have at least two very important relationships to state governments. First, the success of the Hoover Commission has inspired many states— almost half of them — to create "little Hoover" commissions to study organization of state governments. Second, one of the subjects investigated by the Hoover Commission was "Federal-State" relations and the problems in that field, particularly in regard to Federal grants-in-aid and allocation of areas of taxation.

In Illinois we have high hopes for our reorganization commission, which was authorized by the most recent session of the Legislature. Illinois did some pioneering in the study of state government organization when the so-called Lowden report was issued more than thirty years ago. That report and the changes that followed in Illinois had nation-wide recognition and repetition. Two men who pioneered in this field, Charles E. Merriam and Louis Brownlow, also were part of the last great effort to reorganize the executive branch of the Federal Government in 1937, and it was our common misfortune that their efforts foundered on the rocks of partisan politics.

But in the intervening years since the Lowden Report our state government has grown enormously in its functional responsibilities, its personnel and cost. This growth has been typical of all the states. Taken together, they now spend almost six billion dollars annually and employ almost one million people. Largely subject to state laws and partly subject to state supervision are also our 150,000 local governments, which spend some seven billion dollars more per year. Federal expenditures, it is true, far exceed these figures. In 1932 tax collections by all the states together were about the same as the tax collections by the Federal Government—but by 1947 the Federal Government was collecting over six times as much as the states. Nevertheless, if we eliminate Federal military and foreign commitments, expenditures by states and local governments together are comparable in amount of Federal expenditures. Fiscally, and financially, therefore, the states, together with their dependent local governments, share with the Federal Government a very large responsibility for our governmental system and our national economy.

We are all familiar with the growth of Federal and urban functions since the nation's beginning, but we are not all as conscious of the increase in the service and welfare functions of the States. These functions show no promise of abating whether we decide to emphasize the welfare ideas or the enterprise ideas which our great political parties are contending with, or whether we continue to accept a healthy combination of the two.

The states in 1947 spent over one billion dollars for education and almost half a billion dollars for welfare. They are spending more now. We may hesitate to call this the "welfare state," yet we cannot deny that it is the embodiment of a service state. But the services the states perform are by no means limited to welfare. They make vast expenditures for highways and public works, for agriculture and resource conservation, for policing and military functions, for health and medical services.

No longer the constitutional repository of a somewhat evasive type of sovereignty, the American State has become the fulcrum of our political system, occupying a position midway between the Federal Government, with its responsibility for stablizing our national economy, and our local governments which deal largely with day-to-day community affairs. The state is now a vast public enterprise in its own right with a crucial aggregate impact on the political economy of the whole country.

How soundly, how efficiently, how economically, is this public enterprise being managed. If those of you connected with or interested in national government think you have problems, listen to this. How would you like to reconcile the need for an effective, trained state personnel, with a long entrenched tradition of spoils politics? How would you like to operate with a wordy obsolete constitution, which carefully spells out the details of governmental operation and which virtually cannot be amended? What would the Federal Government do if it were operating under an antiquated tax system? And perhaps most important, how would the Citizens Committee for the Hoover Report deal with the lethargy about state government? It isn't hard to stir up excitement about the Marshall Plan or a nation-wide strike or the Atlantic Pact or even the federal budget. But how many persons know what their state governments do for them? How many ask themselves what they would have to pay for the myriad social and economic tasks which the states and their subdivisions perform, if they had to go out and buy those services on the market?

For me the question, how soundly, how efficiently, how economically is the public enterprise known as "Illinois" being run, is not merely an academic question of public administration.

Every policy problem coming before me is accompanied by its associated problems of administration, organization and management. As these problems pile up, I find the following kinds of questions recurring:

What reduction or consolidation can be made in the numerous departments and commissions which now report directly to me, and what new agencies does the State government need in view of the additional functions that have been imposed on it since its last major reorganization.

I am not citing to you the plight of the states simply to get your sympathy or to divert your eye from your primary goal—the National Government. Nor do we Governors think our job is insurmountable. Rather I raise these questions because of the unique role of the states in our Federal system, and because of the close interrelationships between these and national problems.

On all sides today we are concerned about the problem of bigness in government. Most thinking persons of both political parties recognize that there are limits beyond which government spending cannot be pushed. The cooperation from the leaders of both parties in the development of the Hoover Commission Report — this meeting here today — are eloquent evidence of this grave concern. While disagreeing about the nature of specific programs, here and there, we finally are uniting —under the leadership of this Committee — in our determination to see that the money which is spent, is well spent. But I hope no one will forget that an equally important answer to the problem of bigness in Government is our larger Federal System. With forty-eight active, efficient state centers there is little or no danger of too great a consolidation of governmental authority.

Certainly we must recognize that there are fields in which the states can and should receive assistance from the National Government. Certainly we must understand that the states' financial resources are not unlimited. Surely in this industrial age it is apparent that many of the problems of health, housing, education, transportation and employment inexorably flow over state boundaries. The more we expand our economy, the more our problems will become national in their scope. The educational and medical advantages given to the Negro youth in the south, for example, vitally affect us in Illinois. Many of those youths will come to our state, and we will have to bear the burden to the extent that they are badly educated or in poor health. No amount of violent pleading for "states rights" can possibly stop the ever-increasing scope of these national problems.

But on the other hand, those who say that the state is out of date, or becoming so, have forgotten the facts of life about our democratic America.Who organizes and operates our public schools? The states. Who protects the persons and property of our people? In the main, the states. Nor do we want a national code governing persons and property, except in interstate affairs, which no state can cover alone.

Within its constitutional field of action, the commonwealth for a century and a half has been free to work out laws and administrative arrangements adapted to the rich variety of interests and areas in the country. If a state hits upon a good idea, it can quickly be adopted elsewhere, modified, or tried and found wanting. If a state wants to be dry, so be it; or wet, even so. One state even taxes the illegal sale of liquor. A state can have a community property law, or not as it sees fit. It can experiment with various forms of local government in cities and schools as it will, or deal with agriculture or business or labor within wide limits. The state can pass blue sky laws, or regulate public utilities as it sees fit, set up standards for state banks and insurance systems, and experiment with welfare plans. It is well to note that Wisconsin started the unemployment payments later adopted in revised form for the entire country.

This power to pass upon and decide local affairs is one of the very greatest assets of our free society, making possible democratic participation at the grass roots of our human relations. If our one hundred fifty million people did not have states, they would create them, rather than centralize all power at one central point, where congestion of authority would soon defeat the purposes and possibilities of democratic development and progress.

The political genius of the founding fathers recognized the values of home rule on the one hand and national unity on the other, and in our Federal system built even better than they knew.

I suggest these thoughts because there are now some among us who are saying that the states are dead or dying, and that the National Government inexorably is eating up the last vestiges of the Federal system. Many of these persons have failed to consider what the states do, and have failed to realize that failure to perform efficiently on the part of the states has perhaps been the greatest cause of danger to the states.

Too often people fail to remember that "states rights" must be accompanied by states' responsibilities. Many of the problems of "states rights" are caused by "states wrongs". The greatness of a state does not depend on its size, its wealth, its population, but upon the manner in which it helps to make good the ends of government. We Governors have no quarrel with the National Government, but are only in a friendly competition in promoting the pursuit of human happiness, in increasing our production, and in enriching the values of human life for all our people. And this is a joint task of all levels of government.

What then must we do? By all means continue to work to improve the operations of the National Government. Focus the spotlight of public attention in a nonpartisan way on the problems of bigness in government. We must bring people to the realization that government is their responsiblity, that "rights" entail obligations as well. And you must keep the spotlight focused; this is not a one year, two year, or five year job. The problem of bigness in government is here to stay. You can be successful only to the degree that you are persistent.

But also please don't ever forget the states. Help us at home improve our cumbersome governmental machinery. See that in carrying out essential national policies our Congress utilizes to the greatest extent possible these basic, organic, live state units to bring as close to home as possible the actual operations of the national programs.

What then do I suggest? (1) We must recognize the need for cooperation rather than hostility or capitulation between levels of government. (2) We must root out unnecessary duplications in Federal, state, and local services, assigning each to the government most fitted to administer it in the public interest. (3) We should encourage further Federal and state studies to reduce the number of governmental units. And while attacking Federal bureaucracy we shouldn't be politically too timid to attack inefficient, archaic, useless local units and structures in our own back yards. (4) We should expand sound interstate agreements wherever possible. (5) We should press for wise and efficient administration of the Federal grants which are made for national programs, with only those controls which the public interest requires.

I am grateful to the Citizens Committee not only for carrying to the people the importance of the Hoover Commission reports, but for stimulating a general re-awakening of the need for more effective citizen understanding, participation and interest in the problems of government. Then our united effort can go far to see that all levels of government participate in making democracy work. To you who know our problems and can influence our future we turn in hope and for help in simplifying and modernizing our housekeeping practices at home, because too many of us still are doing our laundry by hand.

CONFERENCE ON INDUSTRIAL SAFETY, CHICAGO
December 14

URING THE TIME that I make this short talk to you today there will be at least three Illinois industrial workers killed or injured on the job. It may be someone you know; it may be in a plant you represent; or it may be someone unknown to any of us except as a case before the Industrial Commission. But one worker is injured on the job in Illinois industry on the average of every three minutes of each working day.

At least 90% of these accidents are preventable. The greater part of them occur in plants employing two hundred persons or less, where there is as yet no organized, intelligent program for applying tested safety techniques.

It is our job to reach these plants. I think the situation warrants a greater effort to make the owners and the employees realize the seriousness of the problem. We have the "know how", but it has not been applied in 70% of our industrial plants in Illinois.

I want you people, leaders in your fields, to become missionaries for industrial safety in this state in order that we may reduce industrial accidents to an absolute minimum.

We are all apalled by the horrible destruction of life in wartime, and horrible as that loss is, we should remember that industrial production in peacetime takes a heavy toll also. Certainly we must do everything within our power to work for peace and the settlement of our differences without resort to war; but let us also remember that human life is always dear, whether it is lost on the battlefield or in the factory.

Why have we permitted this unnecessary loss of life and injury in our industrial plants? Why have we allowed this enormous waste of production and man-power to continue.?

Is it because we have not been concerned with human misery? Is it because we take it for granted that injuries and occupational diseases are a necessary part of our industrial life — the cost of which is borne first by the worker, then by industry through loss of production and man-hours of labor, and finally by the state in cases where the loss of income may place the worker or his dependents on public assistance lists? And let us not forget that anything which increases production costs also adds to the prices which consumers pay.

It is my conviction that we simply have not realized the seriousness of the problem. We have a tendency to take these losses all too casually.

I hope this meeting, and the main conference next spring, will emphasize and dramatize the problem of industrial safety in a way that will produce real results. I don't think we need to have a mass slaughter of workers in industry to bring us out of our complacency and make us aware of the tremendous and needless loss of life and limb in our factories.

The State of Illinois appropriates money for factory inspection and for the enforcement of our present laws relating to safety. We appropriate money for the compilation of statistics on industrial accidents. These are necessary. But the compiling of statistics and the best job we can do in our Factory Inspection Division are not sufficient.

We have neither the men nor the money to reach every factory in Illinois.

Even if we had twice as many inspectors and double the appropriation, it would still be neither possible nor desirable to look only to the compulsions of law for the achievement of the maximum degree of safety in industry. That will come only with greater education and with a genuine and widespread will to apply the new knowledge.

Our present meeting is an example of what I mean. We have here a cross-section representing management, labor, and the public; safety organizations, insurance companies, universities, and newspapers. Here is a forum in which worker, employers, public representatives and government officials work together on a problem of common concern to all. It is democracy at its best.

We have made tremendous progress in the field of labor-management relations in the last fifteen or twenty years. Employers and workers have had the experience of meeting on the basis of equality to bargain collectively and to exchange ideas.

Labor-management committees during the war made a real contribution to our war effort. In many places these committees have continued and their functions have become a regular part of day-to-day collective bargaining. Many plants and many unions have safety committees of workers. More should have such committees.

All employers cannot tear down obsolete buildings and replace them with modern, scientifically planned structures, but all can, I am sure, give careful consideration to their present equipment and honestly make an effort to make the very best use of what they have. Aside from providing the best physical equipment possible, and the best supervision, employers are in the best position to know the newest methods and techniques in safety engineering.

In anticipation of the major conference next spring, six technical committees have been created and are now at work. I am sure there will be recommendations made to the April conference which will enable it, in turn, to make valuable suggestions to industry, to the Department of Labor, to me as Governor, and to the Legislature.

I can assure you that the ultimate recommendations will receive the most earnest consideration. We want this to be an active, constructive attempt. We do not want this to be a "do nothing" or a "kind words" endeavor. We want your honest opinions and your studied recommendations.

Illinois will be one of the first states to hold a Governor's Conference on Industrial Safety. Our state ranks third as an industrial state in the nation. Other states will be watching us. They will be interested not only in what we do here today, but even more in what we accomplish between now and the spring conference. They will be anticipating the findings of these various technical committees, and they will be interested in the recommendations made by the main conference in April.

Interest in this conference, however, goes even further. You may be interested in knowing that we are honored at this conference with the presence of government labor officials from Bolivia, Chile, and Costa Rica, and that our Labor Department periodically receives requests from other countries for information on our industrial accident situation and our methods of combating it.

More and more we exchange experiences and ideas with our friends in other countries. If we can come out of this conference with a positive and intelligent plan which will reduce industrial accidents in Illinois, and this is our primary purpose, we may also make a genuine contribution to industrial safety in other states of our own nation, and in other nations of the world.

I am grateful for your help and interest.

1950

S INCE THIS IS YOUR fiftieth Annual Dinner and also the mid-point in our revolutionary twentieth century, I can't resist the temptation of making a few "then and now" observations. I know some chronologists tell us that the second half of the twentieth century will not begin until 1951, and that all mid-century surveys should be deferred for a year. But you may not ask me to speak next year, and besides this is your fiftieth Annual Dinner — and almost my fiftieth annual reminder that life is short and the first fifty years are the hardest — I hope! So you'll forgive me if I reflect a bit about the mid-century and contrast that promise of 1900 with the reality of today and perhaps speculate a bit on the future.

In 1900 America's dominant mood was one of optimism. The Spanish-American War had been gloriously concluded. The United States had reached its present continental limits and was extending its hand across the sea. American imperialists, chanting Kipling's refrain of the "white man's burden", were casting covetous eyes across the Pacific and south of the border. The nation was prosperous. Bank clearings had more than doubled in the five years from 1894 to 1899. We had forged ahead of Great Britain in the value of domestic exports. The western farmers, after a generation of hand-to-mouth existence, had started to make money and were beginning to give some thought to the amenities of life. The old sod house of the Great Plains was being superseded by frame dwellings. The scars of the Civil War were healed. Cotton had become a profitable crop again, and the South had reached a degree of stabilization unknown since ante-bellum days. The railroads felt the new prosperity and earned more money in 1899 than in any previous year.

Perhaps the millenium had not yet dawned, but at least America seemed on the threshhold of a century of unprecedented peace and prosperity.

Well, half of that century is gone, and with it much of our complacent optimism. Our time on earth has been the bloodiest, most disordered and violent since the Renaissance illuminated the Dark Ages. Two world conflagrations and two economic convulsions have taken a savage toll in physical suffering and spiritual disillusionment. Today's mood is one of anxiety. People are apprehensive about tomorrow. Some even ask: "Will there be a tomorrow?"

The specter of Communism, which a century ago Marx and Engels boastfully proclaimed to be "haunting Europe", today actually stalks the world, and with it are the twin specters of war and depression.

Kipling's "white man's burden" is all but forgotten, but mankind cannot but have a feeling akin to remorse as it contemplates the awful relevance of his other refrain: "Lest we forget."

What will the next half century be like? Will it bring a repetition of the frustrations and disasters of the last fifty years on a more appalling scale? Or will we somehow find a way to break the wretched cycle of wars and depressions and end the twentieth century in a golden, peaceful sunset? Will we take advantage of the real, moral, social and scientific advance of the last fifty years to set at rest anxiety and fear?

The answer depends, I suspect, as much or more upon the consecrated efforts of organizations like yours as upon what statesmen and politicians do.

We should not let the wide gulf between the hopes of 1900 and the fears of 1950 fool us into thinking that the last half century was a period of unrelieved regression. It may well be that when the definitive history of the twentieth century is finally written it will record as the most significant development of the first half of the century not the two World Wars nor the great depression, not the Russian Revolution, not the rise and fall of Hitler, not even the atom bomb, but rather the expansion of the intellectual and moral horizons of millions of people, an expansion that has been evidenced in America by two striking developments. First, a recognition of our responsibility as a nation in the world community, and, second, an appreciation of our individual and collective responsibility to alleviate human suffering — a recognition of the correlative truths that we are our brother's keeper and that all men are our brothers.

Our assumption of international responsibilities and our increased concern for the individual human being are closely related. You, more than most people, realize domestic and international problems can't be isolated. Through the Combined Jewish Appeal, you have given concrete recognition to the fact that there is a close relationship between the rebuilding of Jewish life in Europe and Israel and the maintenance of a flourishing Jewish community here in Chicago.

Just as we have discovered that freedom is compounded of economic as well as political elements, so we are learning that morality is made up of social as well as personal elements, and that the two cannot be separated.

Our obligations extend not only to those close to us, but to everyone. Charity begins at home, but it doesn't end there.

These ideas are not new. They were passionately proclaimed by the prophets of Israel and form a basic part of the Judaeo-Christian tradition which underlies western civilization. As Franklin Roosevelt said in his Social Security message to Congress more than fifteen years ago: "Our task of reconstruction does not require the creation of new and strange values. It is rather the finding of the way once more to known, but to some degree forgotten, ideals and values."

In the United States, and most of Western Europe, as Prof. Summer Slichter has noted, the first half of the twentieth century has been an age of remarkable moral progress, with great concern for human well-being and a growing capacity on the part of the community to deal with its problems. When there is so much pessimism, so many forebodings, so many predictions of disaster, it is well to count our blessings.

There has been much talk about "security" of late, as if that word meant only financial security. But man does not live by bread alone, and security involves more than economics. There are needs beyond physical needs —emotional and spiritual needs—that will not be satisfied by acts of the Legislature and of Congress, because security also means a feeling that one has a place in life, a sense of belonging to the community. Older people especially, often feel that there is little left in life for them. Family and community neglect have resulted in too many aged people being committed to our state institutions, but they can do relatively little to assuage the feeling of loneliness that is the lot of so many. You Jewish people, largely I suspect because of your strong tradition of family and community responsibility, have always been leaders in this field. Your Jewish People's Institute and the Home for Aged Jews have made out-standing contributions toward relieving some of these wants which are always so costly to the taxpayer and often so cruel to the individual. I wish more people shared your sense of responsibility for your aged and infirm.

We hear much talk about freedom and security as if it is an "either-or" proposition — you must choose one or the other, but you can't have both. I would present it, rather, as a "both or neither" proposition. When people are insecure, whether their insecurity is economic or psychological, their freedom is an illusion. Conversely, there can be no real security without freedom.

True security can exist only for free men in a free society. That's why all of us — government, individuls and voluntary associations — are working toward the unfinished task of creating a society in which each individual personality will be able to develop itself in accordance with the divine imperative. The democratic form of government cannot survive these perilous times unless it is the genuine expression of a truly democratic society. The Greek city states did not perish from an excess of democracy, but because they were false fronts for a society that was very undemocratic in our sense of the word. At the time of the adoption of our Federal Constitution there were still many undemocratic elements in our social structure. The institution of slavery was the most glaring example, but there were others. Women could not vote, and married women could not own property. Workers were often at the mercy of their employers.

We have made much progress since that time — slavery has been abolished; women have been emancipated; the principle of collective bargaining has been recognized. But there is still much to be done. So long as there is discrimination in employment on account of race, color or religion, so long as many of our citizens are deprived of basic human rights, our task of creating a democratic society is unfinished. Those who seek to use our democratic processes to perpetuate the undemocratic remnants of a dead past, are I fear, courting disaster.

Today we are engaged with the Kremlin in a struggle for the hearts and minds of men. We condemn Communism and its materialistic philosophy. But, if our only advantage over Russia is our superiority in material things, if we counter Soviet materialism only with a materialism of our own, the world will find little to choose between us.

We denounce Communism for its godlessness, and rightly so. But if our only god is the gadget, wherein is our advantage? You can't fight a shooting war without bullets, and you can't fight a war of ideologies without ideas.

We won't resist the Soviet impact on the Western world with a schizophrenic society which protests its devotion to democratic ideals while it indulges in undemocratic practices, or which recoils in horror from an alien materialism but, blinded by its own material accomplishments, loses sight of its spiritual heritage. If Western civilization is to save its body, it must save its soul too.

In the words of Dr. Charles Malik, the Delegate of Lebanon to the United Nations:

> If the Western world can show a way to eradicate the shame, the scandal, of poverty, of exploitation, of oppression, of greed, without resort to social revolution and class struggle and dictatorship, if it can place these material values within their proper place within the context of a mighty spiritual

movement which will be revolutionary without being subversive and which will draw its substance from the infinite riches of the Western positive tradition, then communism will vanish, and the specter which now walks the earth will be laid forever.

That's why the task of discovering and maintaining,the proper relationship between the individual and society is always so important; that's why we must continue the moral progress of the last half century; and that's why the work of ogranizations like yours will influence the outcome of the next fifty years.

During the last fifty years we have heard the issue of the twentieth century variously described as Democracy versus Kaiserism, self-determination versus despotism, Democracy versus Fascism, Democracy versus Communism, and religion versus materialism. Accurate as each of these labels may be, they are but different facets of the major issue of this and every other century —the relation of the individual to society. For no man can live to himself — and certainly not in the twentieth century.

Some of you may recall the address on a letter that figured in Thorton Wilder's play *Our Town,* a little more than a decade ago. This is the address: "Jane Crofut, the Crofut Farm, Grover's Corners, Sutton County, New Hampshire, United States of America, Continent of North America, the Earth, the Solar System, the Universe, the Mind of God."

The address contains some truths the postman probably didn't appreciate. For each of us, whether named Jane Crofut or John Doe, is a human personality with his own hopes and fears and aspirations, and with a mixture of strength and weakness that makes up an individual character. But we must live with our fellows in Grover's Corners or in Springfield or in Chicago. And it can't stop there, for we are part of the great company of humankind. All of us are fellow passengers on this planet, and we realize as never before that our destiny is inseparably linked. As John Donne wrote long ago: "No man is an island, entire of itself; every man is a piece of the continent, a part of the main."

But the address on the letter went even beyond the world —to the Mind of God. And that's what gives meaning to this seemingly hopeless and confused maze of interrelationships.

Man is not only an individual. As Seneca observed, he is also a social animal. But he is something more than an animal. He is endowed by his Creator with inalienable rights. He is a moral agent with the power of making choices affecting not only himself, but countless others. It is because we are more than animals that we can blow ourselves off the face of this planet in the next fifty years. It is also because we are more than animals that we can make this world a better place — better both in material things and in the things of the spirit — than it has ever been before.

In concert with our fellows we can make things happen, and I think it is time we stopped shivering with fear of what is going to happen to us and started thinking about what we are going to make happen.

Just as you have built this great organization to relieve the sorrows of your people, so all of us, working together, unafraid to translate good will into action, can do much to bring reality to the golden promises of our century.

50TH ANNIVERSARY BANQUET
PARENT-TEACHER ASSOCIATION, CHICAGO
April 20

I HAVE A KEEN PERSONAL interest in being here tonight as you celebrate the rounding out of fifty years as an organization devoted to the improvement of the schools of Illinois. I welcome the opportunity to commend you, officially and personally, for the work you are doing now and have done through the years for the welfare of all the children of this state. I am proud that my own grandmother, Letitia Green Stevenson, was a pioneer in this work. I am proud that she was among those who brought into existence the organization that was forerunner of the present National Congress of Parents and Teachers, and also was one of the founders and first officers of the Illinois PTA Congress. I know how proud she would be that this organization has achieved such size (356,000 members in Illinois), influence and prestige as it enjoys today. And honesty compels me to add that I also know how surprised she would be to see me here tonight in this honored and very exposed position!

When she and a comparatively small group of women met in Washington in February 1897 and formed the first National Congress of Mothers they could scarcely have envisioned that there would ever emerge an organization numbering its national membership in the millions. Mrs. Alice Birney, who was first president of the National Congress of Mothers, is credited with the idea which inspired the organization. She had asked herself the question: "How can the mothers be educated and the nation made to recognize the supreme importance of the child?" She found that many, many other women throughout America were eager to find the answer to that same question.

She was able to interest a number of them in coming together in the nation's capital to pool their thoughts and efforts in that direction. Sixteen women were present at the meeting from Illinois. As its name implied, the National Congress of Mothers originally was limited to parents. But soon afterward the organization opened its membership to teachers and became the Parents and Teachers Association, and ultimately the Congress of Parents and Teachers.

Mrs. Roger McMullen of Evanston was selected as organizer for Illinois, and in May of 1900 the first Illinois Congress of Parents and Teachers was held. Mrs. McMullen was chosen President and my grandmother Stevenson was elected one of three Vice Presidents. I know she always looked upon this as a great honor, and that in a full and active life she regarded the work of the PTA as one of the most gratifying tasks she ever undertook.

Now that we have observed its growth and are able to assess its work over a long period of time, we all recognize that the PTA has been one of the most effective forces in raising the standards of our public schools and marshalling support for public education. I think it would be no exaggeration to say that the remarkable growth and development of the free educational system in this country could not have come about, and certainly could not have reached its present stage of advancement, without the energy and influence of the Parent-Teacher Associations throughout America.

So I heartily congratulate the Illinois Congress on its fiftieth birthday. As you contemplate the distance you have traveled and the milestones you have reached in the last half century, I hope you will be able to gain fresh inspiration and vigor to carry on in the years ahead. If I didn't know your organization well, I might caution you against spending too much time looking backward at the past rather than looking forward to the tasks ahead. But I don't think there is any danger of that in your case. I have had experience with too many PTA delegations to have any doubts whatever about the determination and persuasiveness of a group of women who know what they want and are out to get it!

There is logic, of course, in considering the meaning of past events in planning any future course of action. And in planning for the future of the schools I think we would do well to thoroughly understand the significance of our free educational system in the light of history. Sometimes I think that we fail to grasp the real significance to be found in the evolution of America in the last century and a half. I am not referring to our great material advancement, the conquest of a continent, the dramatic achievement of a new pioneering scientific knowledge, or the raising of the standard of living of all the people, remarkable as all these have been.

Rather, I am referring to the fact that we in this country have given to the world a demonstration that men and women can work together, under a free government, to widen the opportunities for all of them for a richer, more fruitful life. Here in America we have demonstrated that a government by the people and for the people can be preserved and flourish in a century that has seen two global wars and a shattering revolution.

President Conant, of Harvard, recently said that America's greatest contribution to the development of civilization has not been in abstract thought, in literature or in any of the arts. It has been, as he phrased it, "a demonstration that a certain type of society long dreamed of by idealists can be closely approached in reality — a free society in which the hopes and aspirations of a large fraction of the members find enduring satisfaction through outlets once reserved for only a small minority of mankind."

Few would deny that the unique success of the American experiment owes more to our system of free public schools than to any other factor. The vast educational system which we have built up has proved to be an instrument for forwarding our democracy, and an expression of the idealism which is the essence of the spirit of this republic. To have had a substantial part in building and advancing that educational system, as your organization has had for the last half century, is to have performed a highly valuable service for our own and future generations.

But the task of education in America, in Illinois, in your home community, is by no means finished. In a sense it has barely begun. As our population grows, as our economy becomes more complex, as this nation assumes a larger role in world affairs, the tasks of education become even greater. If it is indeed true that our system of public education is at once the shield and sword of our ideas and our greatest contribution to Western civilization, then the future of education is all the more significant. In the light of the grim ideological struggle of our times it is all the more essential that our schools adapt themselves to the new responsibilities that we face.

At this mid-century point, professional educators and laymen alike are reappraising our public schools. Fortunately, in few places has there been greater interest in assessing the adequacy of the schools than here in Illinois. That interest has been reflected in many ways. I want to consider for a moment some of the most important of these.

I think the most dramatic steps forward that have been taken in education in this state in recent years can be summarized briefly under three headings:

First, we have made spectacular progress in reorganization of the school districts in Illinois. Since 1945, their number has been reduced from 11,955, to 4,950 as of September 1st, 1949. This unprecedented trend in consolidation of weak districts, and elimination of inadequate schools is still going on.

Second, tremendous improvement has been made in school financing. The increase in state funds for the common schools between 1946 and 1951 will amount to 209 per cent. For the present biennium, the increase in state aid was more than 52 percent. A forumula was devised to encourage better local support of the schools and the more efficient use of the funds, an accomplishment of which I am personally very proud. The new state aide forumula is more realistic in equalizing the comparative income of the schools in poor and rich districts. In addition, the people in scores of local districts throughout Illinois have voted to increase local taxes for schools. And in some, I am happy to say, they have even found it possible to reduce taxes.

In advocating an Illinois school plan for the future, I am not suggesting any Utopian scheme to saddle new burdens on the taxpayers. I do not have in mind fixing goals that we would try to reach overnight. It might require a decade, or in some instances two decades to bring the majority of our schools up to the standards which by reasonable yardsticks would be classified as good. We would have to work toward them a step at a time.

What I visualize is a realistic, practical, attainable set of school standards to be reached in orderly progression. For example, the present reorganization of rural school districts is jeopardized in many areas by poor rural roads, and before that problem can be finally solved we must deal with the highway deficiency. Other preliminary steps involve perfecting the structure of school organization and finance. And before we can ever hope to reach the long-range goals we will need more aggressive leadership, both among the professional educators and laymen, to acquaint all the people with the aims of the program and the benefits that would flow from it.

There are other problems which obstruct our view. We will not be engulfed by the high tide of the wartime baby crop for several years. Will we be ready when it comes? And how about the supply of good, well-trained teachers which is still running short of the demand, although, I'm happy to say, teaching as a profession is becoming more attractive and resuming its rightful place in our society again. I can think of no more worthwhile activity for the PTA than its constant encouragement of our most promising boys and girls to go into teaching as a career.

ANNUAL MEETING OF THE INSURANCE FEDERATION OF ILLINOIS, CHICAGO
April 28

WE TAKE THE DEPARTMENT of Insurance, which attracts so little public attention, very seriously in this administration in Springfield, because insurance affects directly or indirectly nearly all of our eight and a half million citizens. Illinois is a big corn state, a big meat state, a big railway state, a big industrial, a big coal, a big oil state. It also seems to me that we raise an enormous crop of politicians! But the man in the street doesn't realize that Illiois is also a great insurance state. As you gentlemen who represent that enormous business in all its aspects know so well, there are more than 1100 companies licensed to do insurance business in Illinois, and more than 100,000 licensed agents, brokers, solicitors and other insurance specialists. The total premium bill paid by Illinois policy holders exceeds a billion dollars annually.

As I see it, our job is to see to it that every one of those policyholders gets his money's worth and that every company is sound financially. The protection of policyholders is a major function of state government and I shudder to think of the disaster that could befall my administration and the people of this state if the Insurance Department with such an enormous responsibility was not well run.

You can see then why I feel so indebted to the Director and his associates in the Department, and to you of the Insurance Federation of Illinois. It is by your understanding of the problems which confront us and by an earnest, honest, mutual effort to solve them — not selfishly for a particular group, but broadly for the best interest of both the public and industry — that you and the Insurance Department can build and are building a structure of intelligent insurance legislation and regulation here in Illinois.

Mr. Hershey informs me about every other day that he is not satisfied with the Department; that it must be strengthened here and there, and that he has difficulty attracting the men he needs at the salaries he can pay. But that's a familiar refrain to me, and personally I feel that, while we have not been able to accomplish as much as we would like, we have made some noteworthy progress in the past fifteen months. We made some significant changes in the law during the last session of the legislature which was already in session and waiting for us, under our barbaric practice, when we took office last year. Automobile insurance rates have been reduced at a saving to the public of some three million annually; Illinois has been the first to introduce the short form of application for license renewals, fees for examinations have been instituted, and many other reforms and changes. Finally, I can't overlook, nor should you, that Mr. Hershey, who was once a candidate for Governor of Illinois, has operated the Insurance Department with more regard for efficiency and economy than for politics. He has reduced the cost of operating the Department by almost $200,000 a year by administrative reforms and eliminating some thirty unnecessary employees. At which point I am obliged to remind some of you who suffer from the prevalent current delusion that thrift is the peculiar property of one particular political party that Mr. Hershey was Democratic candidate for Governor!

We have another state activity under way of interest to fire insurance people which I am very hopeful will yield important results in time. The tragic fire at the Effingham Hospital a year ago invited public attention to the lack of any comprehensive fire prevention regulations outside of a few of our large cities. To meet this need the legislature enacted legislation which we recommended and the State Fire Marshal, Pat Kelly, has worked out a code with the assistance of a committee of fire prevention experts. It is now under consideration by a committee I've appointed from the public, commerce, industry and labor. I am hopeful that it can be promulgated during the summer and that at last we will have some standards of reasonable fire prevention to protect citizens in the downstate communities where combustible multiple occupancy buildings are constantly increasing.

There is one respect in which we have failed, however, which I must mention because it is your problem and a very serious problem too, that I refuse to believe the industry cannot and will not solve. Repeated complaints come to us about the inability of negroes to obtain insurance coverage on the south side of Chicago. I have spent many hours on this problem and Director Hershey and his staff many weeks, but it remains unsolved. I know the insurance fraternity deny any unfair discrimination. But I also know that there are situations which are hard otherwise to explain. For example, a Negro risk may be insured during the time a loan is outstanding on his premises, but when the loan is retired, some complaints have reached us that the risk is not desired by the particular insurance company. There is, of course, much to be said on both sides of this controversy. The Department staff have held many meetings with the parties concerned and with responsible company and agency representatives in an effort to remove the causes for such charges of unfair discrimination, but the situation persists. It is not only unfair but very unwise. Cases of discrimination can give an underserved black eye to the whole insurance business. I bespeak, therefore, your earnest and prompt recognition of this responsibility. It must be met and this problem solved if you are to prevent an attempt by legislation to stamp out this type of unfair discrimination. As this enlightened industry has met boldly and decisively so many problems in the past, I know it can solve this one which is weighted with such sociological and human importance.

And speaking of legislation, I was happy to note that the Circuit Court of Appeals in St. Louis upheld the constitutionality of the regulatory provisions of Public Law 15 and declared that the Sherman Act is not applicable to cooperative action among insurers in rate-making and related matters to the extent that they are regulated by state law. I hope this decision is sustained and the threat of federal regulation of the insurance business can be forstalled. But in the long run it can be, as in most everything else, only if the industry and the state insurance administrators cooperate wholeheartedly to make state regulation effective. I'm sure no one recognizes the vital and direct stake of all of us in vigorous, scrupulous state governments more clearly than you insurance people.

And that brings me to what I really wanted to talk about a little today —not insurance which you know more about than I'll ever know, but your state government which I think you should know more about. So you'll pardon me, I hope, if instead of talking about the importance of the insurance business to Illinois I try to sell you on the importance of Illinois to the insurance business, and to businessmen generally.

While I'm thankful for the increased concern for state government on the part of the insurance profession, I can't help observing that it illustrates two common and disturbing attitudes toward government. One is the tendency to regard government — all government — as a necessary evil, and to prefer state regulation only because it is considered a little less obnoxious than federal control. When Moran and Mack were going strong in vaudeville as the "Two Black Crows," one of them would pull a harmonica out of his pocket and start to play a wheezy tune. The other would scowl in distaste and say: "Boy, even if dat wuz good I wouldn't like it." Some people are like that about government. Even if it was good they wouldn't like it.

Another conspicuous human trait is to take no interest in one's government until it does something that has a direct and adverse personal effect. Many property owners, for example, pay no attention to their

government until they receive their tax bills. Many insurance men, I suspect, were jolted into realizing the importance of state government only
by the imminent threat of federal regulation. And many people, including
far too many businessmen, still are not alive to the necessity of taking an
active and intelligent interest in the problems of their state. After all, it's
your government, just as the insurance business is your business, and
what it does or doesn't do vitally affects you.

Unfortunately, the states are the most neglected level of government.
People are preoccupied with the national and international scene, naturally enough, and they are interested in their local government because of
its nearness to them. The states, the fulcrum of our political system,
occupying a position between the local governments with their responsibility for day-to-day community housekeeping, and the federal government with its responsibility for stabilizing our national economy, are
often overlooked. But the states are tremendously important. They are
spending a lot of money — about six billion annually — and employing
about a million people. Largely subject to state laws and state supervision
are 150,000 local governments, which spend some seven billion more per
year. Indeed, if you eliminate national defense and foreign expenditures,
the states and local governments together spend about as much as the
federal government.

Even more important is the tone — the moral tone — of state government, which has such a vast influence upon the whole political scene.
Government can never be much stronger than the average of its parts,
and the states are the most important parts. Total diplomacy and total
effort in the cold war can't be effective abroad if they are ineffective at
home. We won't win friends and influence people by mouthing pious
platitudes about the virtues of a democratic people's government. We
must practice what we so loudly preach.Unfortunately, it's sometimes
easier to fight for one's convictions than to live up to them. If we would
command the respect and invite the emulation of peoples all over the
world, we must devote ourselves unsparingly to the grueling day-by-day
task of making our government work on all levels.

We need more responsible people — perhaps more insurance men — to
know, explore and understand our state government. It's a gigantic business, employing some 32,000 persons and spending half a billion dollars a
year. Government in Illinois has become big business, and if it's to be run
efficiently it must have the best possible management. At the top I've got
it — men like Harry Hershey. But it isn't easy to recruit top-flight
managerial talent at the salaries we pay in Illinois. You can get good men

only on the basis of unselfish public service. And too often the reward for such sacrificial service is not gratitude in lieu of dollars, but criticism, misunderstanding and abuse.

And I hasten to add that the Director of Insurance is the exception that proves the rule. Instead of the customary brickbats, he seems to be getting lots of bouquets tossed his way and I'm glad to at least scent the aroma!

I would ask you as responsible businessmen and as citizens of Illinois, to take a broad view of government — to try to understand the entire picture, not simply the part of it that deals directly with your own business. That's why, instead of speaking just about insurance, I wanted to talk with you about a few of the most urgent problems confronting our state government.

We are going through a transition period in state government. The war and postwar years of abnormally high state income are over and we have entered upon an era of realism in the economic affairs of the state. Instead of having more money in the treasury than could be spent we now are going to have trouble making ends meet, in spite of rigid economies. The problems that were deferred so long because of the depression and the war have caught up with us, and we can defer them no longer.

It's easy to say "damn the spenders," but you don't save any money that way. If the energy that goes into unreasoning damnation were concentrated on ways and means, we might get somewhere. An uneducated resentment is never effective for positive good, but understanding and a positive objective are. Certainly I would welcome your interest in this intricate and emotional subject of budgets and taxes because I know that regardless of your political affiliations, regardless of the fact that you are in private life and I happen to be in politics at the moment, we both want the same things for Illinois.

Besides, I need a lot of help if I am going to accomplish what you hired me to do. And you can help most if you understand the whole problem, not just the fraction or portion of it that appears to most affect you, because it all affects us and it affects us all. Government is the biggest business there is, and you are all in it whether you like it or not, and its hand is in your pocket day and night. I am firmly convinced that the conscientious public official confronted with inertia, prejudice or cynicism on the part of private citizens finds that state of mind a larger hurdle to clear than the open opposition of those who make politics their profession.

How anyone with a grade school education can any longer be indifferent to government from a purely self-interested, material point of view is beyond me, let alone from any ideological and abstract considerations of principle. We hear a lot about government interference with business. But I submit that one of the reasons there has been a trend toward wider and wider governmental authority is that too many people have shunned politics as something beneath their dignity, and have refused to take any part in it. A shocking percentage of businessmen, for example, don't even bother to vote in elections.

I hope I've persuaded some of you at least that the State government of Illinois is worth some of your time and close attention, that we are trying to clean up and trying to peel off the old layers of bureaucracy, waste, tradition, obstruction and venality. Like the preacher said — "we're working to beat hell."

CENTRAL REGIONAL CONFERENCE OF THE CIVIL SERVICE ASSEMBLY OF THE UNITED STATES AND CANADA, SPRINGFIELD
May 2

WHEN I FIRST DISCOVERED that I was to speak to you on the place of civil service in a democracy, I was somewhat self-conscious about the broad sweep of my subject. There is a tendency, in these trying times, to try to relate every conceivable topic to the central issue of the proper political organization of society. But it is done too often by main strength and not by logic.

I do not really feel, however, that the effect in this instance is far-fetched. And I am certain that you who are devoting your lives to perfecting the interaction of the two concepts agree with me. Your participation in the Civil Service Assembly, which has done so much for good government, evidences your faith in the contribution of good personnel policy and public administration.

We of the western world persevere in our allegiance to democracy because we believe it is good government. Good, fundamentally because it has the largest room for personal freedom and respect for individual dignity; good because it maintains this scope at the same time that it performs those essential functions of government which are the hall-marks of western civilization.

Unless we continue firmly in this belief, the free world will disappear. Unless we communicate this conviction to others, the free world can be engulfed. And unless the integrity of this belief is unimpaired, we shall falter in the long struggle before us.

I think that, in temporal as in spiritual matters, faith is most securely founded on works. The strength and the durability of our convictions about democratic government will be determined in the main by demonstrations of its capacity to do its job well. Anything which bears upon that capacity is related to the ominous circumstances in which democracy now finds itself. Since nothing can be more intimately related to the way in which a task is done than the people who do it, we must consider the civil service principle in the broadest perspective.

In my inaugural address as Governor of Illinois, I said: "Government, however good the laws, will not rise above the quality of the men who comprise it." Having thus placed laws and men in their proper relationship, I promptly proceeded to become almost completely preoccupied with laws, not with men! But this was not due to the familiar separation of words from deeds by public officials, but rather to the awkward practice we have in Illinois, thanks to our Constitution, of having the Legislature assembled in Springfield to greet the incoming Governor and in general session throughout the first six months of his term.

Despite this precipitous plunge into an unfamiliar, hazardous sea, some important landfalls were made in the legislative area affecting public personnel. Indeed, it has been said that not since 1905 when Illinois, following upon the heels of New York and Massachusetts, first adopted a civil service act has any session of the General Assembly enacted as much forward-looking legislation relating to state employees.

Good democratic government has more than one foundation. Not the least of these are active, vigorous, aggressive political parties — not too many parties, but at least two! The role played by party organizations in bringing about participation in pulic affairs, popular interest in issues and informed discussion is, in my judgment, underestimated. It is fashionable to disparage organized political partisanship as having no aims or values other than narrowly selfish purposes, many of which cluster about the patronage system.

In the last year and a half, I have learned a great deal about political parties. At the risk of even greater understatement, I have learned a great deal about the so-called spoils system. As to the former, my conviction has grown that political organization is indispensable to effective democratic government. And, although I have not altered my views about the waste and inefficiency of patronage systems, I understand better than ever before their relationship to the continuous operation of our indispensable two-party system.

It is a truism that in this world we seldom get something for nothing. The patronage method of job dispensation is a substantial part of the price we have paid for the organized party activity which is vital in a democracy. The level of our political maturity, or rather immaturity, has been such that strong and, above all, immediately tangible incentives have been necessary to secure participation in party work. A job on the public payroll is the most compelling inducement possible, or so it has seemed in our development as a self-governing people. The party managers have been discerningly practical sociologists. They have made, in the main, an accurate, albeit unflattering and sometimes unconscious, appraisal of what is required to make political parties tick and thereby serve the larger purposes of democratic government. Perhaps the net result has been that a greater amount of good has come from a lesser amount of evil.

But evil there undeniably is, certainly in the sense of too wide a margin of incompetence, inefficiency and wasteful turnover. As a people, I think we are committed to a philosophy of the perfectibility of our political instincts as of our morals. I believe that our capacities for self-government grow and change for the better in common with our economic, our cultural, and our scientific advancements. If I am in error, then the outlook for democracy in this period of peril is dark indeed.

Our problem is not, therefore, merely to explain the inevitable collisions between the highest standards of public personnel administration, on the one hand, and the needs of party organization on the other. It is, rather, for us to seek a formula for further improvement.

With the growth of government at all levels, competence and economy must come first, and if political parties don't deliver better, more scrupulous public administration all along the line, the people will change managers. All of which bodes well, it seems to me, for the career concept of public service. Stated in the most cynical way, it must come more and more not because political managers won't surrender wider areas of patronage, but because the people will demand it and the wisest political manager gets for the people what they demand before they get him.

But there is apparently opening up another avenue of escape from this dilemma. It is not the path of compromise of the merit system or of dilution of sound personnel practices which have been so laboriously fought for and achieved over the years. It involves no surrender to those unenlightened professional political leaders — who claim a vested interest in the spoils system and lack both the imagination and the will to devise newer methods of stimulating political interest and activity more in keeping with the times.

I point instead to the brightening horizon of wider political awareness, of increased popular recognition of the worth of participation in party

activity. This greater awakening to the issues of the day will be accompanied by a desire to do something about them. This ought, in turn, to lead to
efforts to accomplish results through the parties. I would in short, like to
see more people ringing doorbells because they believe in men and measures; and not merely because they hope to be rewarded by a routine job. I
think the time has come to pay our citizens the compliment of assuming
that they have grown up and away from the old incentives. Whether or
not this assumption is premature, surely we should be setting our faces in
the direction of making it a reality.

In the attainment of public office, I would prefer to see the incentives
increased rather than lessened. By this I mean that the jobs where policy is
made — where power resides to put principles into practice — should be
available to those who have served their party apprenticeship. If they are
the right people to begin with, they will, I submit, possess superior qualifications for the important posts. They will have a knowledge of the infinite
intricacies of government in operation and a background of close contact
with the electorate.

Nothing has exasperated me more than to be told that I ought not to
consider appointing a particular person to a particular job solely because
he has been active in a political party. The issue should be not whether the
individual has interested himself in normal and healthy activities, but
whether he is honest, competent and qualified for the job. What, I inquire,
is to happen to the quality of our political leadership if party activity
becomes a bar instead of a step to public office, a badge of second class
citizenship? The idea that because a man has been active in party politics
he must be disqualified for public office is a dangerous myth and a sad
reflection on the state of our thinking about democratic government.

Political participation should be encouraged, not discouraged. The
young businessman may well find an evening a week spent in party activity fully as rewarding as one passed with his colleagues in some club or
organization dedicated to criticism but not participation. The housewife
with some time on her hands may derive as much satisfaction from performing a party assignment as attending a bridge club. And, when the
elections are over, these people will be content with seeing the things they
believe in come into being without any desire to displace someone in a
public job which ought never to be subject to the ebb and flow of political
tides.

Let us, I say, work towards the lessening of patronage pressures by
broadening the base of party participation. The necessary corollary of this
is, of course, the steady extension and strengthing of career service in the

non-policy making positions, whether they be routine or highly skilled. Let us, at the same time, put to work in political activity in its best sense, the increasing numbers of our fellows who, due to the stresses of the past and the apprehensions of the future, are moved to stop playing the ostrich about a citizens' government and to start fighting for its greater glory.

WESTERN STATE TEACHERS COLLEGE COMMENCEMENT EXERCISES, MACOMB
June 1

I HAVE BEEN REFLECTING — all too briefly as you will soon learn — about what I should say here today: whether to talk of the conflict between collectivism and individualism, East and West, Communism and Democracy, or whatever you choose to call it, which is so popular because it is so non-controversial, and which is so tiresome because it is so well understood. I discarded that, tempting though it was to talk piously and wisely about experiences inside the Soviet Union and inside international conferences with Eastern Europeans who have different convictions — and sometimes they are convictions — about the duty and destiny of mankind.

Then for a moment I took refuge — comfortable, confident refuge — in the subject of government, with which I am mightily concerned these days, and the imperative necessity for more awareness, more active, disinterested participation by privileged people like you. Unhappily, it occurred to me, that in the last couple of years I had already said about everything I could think of on that subject. So I discarded that, and half a dozen other ideas, and concluded to talk to you a little about education, in which you are interested and in which every thinking adult must be interested if he cherishes any hope.

Actually, I suppose it makes little difference what I talk about, because you won't remember what I say, even if it's important, which it isn't, any more than I remember what a large cultivated gentleman said on a hot June day before you were born, when I graduated. I can't even remember his name.

Indeed I sometimes wonder why we have commencement addresses at all. After all the lectures you've listened to for the past several years this last ordeal seems a little gratuitous. I can see some justification for this final assault of piety and wisdom on the helpless in the privately endowed colleges, particularly if their endowment needs replenishing. A commencement speaker is always flattered and if he's rich and gets an honorary degree there's at least a sporting chance the the University will get some money in the fullness of time.

But I can't see much advantage to the practice in tax supported institutions like Western, unless it is to afford pompous governors a chance to show off their wisdom — or expose their ignorance — which is what makes me actually uncomfortable!

At all events, like the capitalist which I'm not, or the scholar which I'm not, or the Governor, which I am, I'm very much flattered to be asked here today. And, having discarded ideological conflict, participation in government, the state of public morals, the good life, and sundry other subjects about which I know more or less, I want to talk about teaching and education about which I know distinctly less — I'll probably talk about all the other things I've discarded in the process!

I want to talk about teaching and education because most of you have dedicated yourselves to the useful and difficult vocation of teaching, and therefore I consider you very important people.

You are very important people because you are going to be teachers, entrusted with the processing of the most precious of all our resources, human minds and personalities. You will have the opportunity to produce the most valuable of products —happy, useful lives. You will have to contend with the challenging inquiry and intellectual confusion which are the fruit of the conflict of ideas in our time. The measure of progress which you can achieve in dissipating false concepts and advancing wise ones is dependent on the resourcefulness and energy you bestow upon your chosen profession.

Progress in the quest for truth and for happy, useful lives depends also on our vast public school system of which many of you will be a part. That system is at once the manifestation of the idealism of our republic and the vehicle on which free democratic society moves forward. As Dr. Conant of Harvard said:

> We have dreamed for generations of a type of society never seen in the world before — a society in which the ideals of liberty and equality have real meaning because they are regarded as social goals. Each decade we are anxious to move nearer to those goals.
>
> By this desire and our evaluation of the success or failure of our efforts, we give content to the ideals summed up by such phrases as 'the maximum of personal freedom,' 'the minimum of class distinction,' 'tolerance of diversity among individuals and creeds,' 'civil liberties,' and above all 'equality of opportun-

ity for all American youth.' These beliefs have been the mainspring of the amazing development of our free tax-supported schools. To the extent these schools continue strong we may have confidence in the vigor of our American traditions; to the degree the effectiveness of public education is increased, we may be hopeful that the oncoming generations will be committed to American ideals and equipped to develop still further this unique society of free men.

There are unmistakable signs of a reawakened interest in our public school system, hopeful, encouraging signs. A National Citizens Commission for the public schools has been organized, federal aid to the schools is being considered by Congress, here in Illinois the last session of the legislature dealt far more generously with the schools than ever before in history. We have made spectacular progress in school district reorganization and consolidation. In five years the number of Illinois school districts has been reduced by more than half, which means better financed, larger and better equipped schools. A highly qualified commission is at work now to further improve the organization, efficiency and financing of the Illinois system. The training of teachers is improving and broadening. Teachers' salaries are rising. These are heartening signs, and what is going on here is going on in greater or lesser degree all over the country.

I have always felt that one of the hardest problems faced by public officials is the indifference of so many people to details and facts about our government — their own government. I think one of the greatest achievements of the last two decades, commencing with the depression of the early Thirties, has been the awakening of the many millions of American men and women to a larger interest in and understanding of their governments — local, state and federal. It would be hard to prove, but I nonetheless believe it to be true, that everywhere people are today taking a greater interest in decent government, in forward-looking government than before. Perhaps it could even be said that the famous words about fooling the people are infinitely more true than when Lincoln uttered them back in the 1860's. Two world wars in a generation and crushing taxes have had their effect.

I think the same is true of our attitude toward education. The statistics on our progress in the past fifty years are impressive. In 1890 only one out of fourteen children between the ages of 14 and 17 was in school. Today the proportion has grown to four out of five. The number of high school graduates has been increasing since the turn of the century about thirteen times as fast as the population and the number of college graduates six times as fast. No longer do we look upon a college education as a luxury. Parents are taking a keener interest in the schools their children attend. They are more interested in the teachers who teach their children and in their curricula.

As long as we have this keen interest in education, not only is your profession more attractive but we can keep pace with the growth and the change which are the law of life. We will be spurring the eternal search for truth, and teaching the truth that will keep men free. We will be building our youth for the future, even though we cannot always build the future for our youth.

Speaking of the future, I think few would confess satisfaction with the condition of public school education in America and I am glad that both in Illinois and elsewhere, conscientious, competent appraisal of programs and facilities is going forward. Any appraisal, however, is confronted with the importance of keeping American society fluid and the manifold local differences which condition educational tasks. To overlook the factors which distinguish one community from another would hinder better public education. The iron hand of uniformity and standardization obliterates diversity and points not in the direction of free inquiry in a free society but in the direction of thought control which we abhor. Hence, appraisals and federal programs, to be healthy and effective, cannot be too far removed from the localities.

The doctrine of equality of educational opportunity is basic to all considerations of American education. We must keep wide open the gates of opportunity to the talented. But it seems to me sometimes that our college product, if anything, may be getting too large rather than too small. Certainly one of the crying needs is to locate the young person of high intellectual ability and prepare him adequately for university work. On the other hand, we know quite well that there is grave danger in exposing too many students of medium ability to the long course of study in our universities and professional schools. It is quite possible to turn out too many highly trained people, for employment in some professional areas we must admit is limited. And it is possible to spend too much money attempting to highly educate the highly uneducable. The two-year college may be the best medium for the post high school education of many students, no matter what their financial status or family background. On the other hand, opportunities and the resources to take advantage of them must be available to help students of outstanding ability to undertake the long years of university work.

There are many questions we must ask about the quality of our schools.

Taking account of flexibility and variation in local conditions we can always apply certain tests: Are students of high intellectual ability being identified and guided into proper channels? Are those with artistic, graphic, and musical talents afforded an opportunity to develop? Is the average student being provided with a program lively and imaginative enough to keep his interest high? Is the vocational training sufficiently broad to give a basis for subsequent choice of occupations? Is it realistically related to the employment situation in the localities, or are students being led up blind alleys?

I would suggest that of very first importance is general education for responsible living, for emotional stability in a complex urbanized society. In an era of ascendancy for the exact sciences, the study of the humanities, of art, literature and history, we should not forget, introduces the student to riches from which he or she can draw life-long satisfaction — and perhaps even help us control the population of our mental institutions.

Obviously there is no easy answer to any of these questions. My point is that they are questions which you as teachers must everlastingly ask and seek to answer, locally, within the neighborhood of your life and work, and with realistic relevance to your students and their families. And bear in mind that if there is race prejudice, lawlessness, disrespect for individual dignity and intolerance of diversity, in your school, it is a reflection not upon the student alone but upon the school as well.

It has fallen to our lot as it did to the ancient Greeks in their time, and to the Romans in theirs, to make a unique contribution to human history. What is that contribution? I would say it was the realization of an idealist's dream of a free society in which hopes and aspirations once reserved for the few are the property of the many. The American system of public education is both the symbol and the means of our great contribution. To show us the way to this concept of democratic society is the aim of the teacher. So, perhaps you will perceive why I think you are very important people.

I remember what an eager young man who had just received his diploma at a theological seminary said: "I am now ready to do the Lord's work, wherever it may lead me, providing it is honorable!"

And to you who are about to teach I recommended what William Lyon Phelps said:

"In my mind, teaching is not merely a life work, a profession, an occupation, a struggle. It is a passion. I love to teach as a painter loves to paint, as a singer loves to sing, as a musician loves to play. Teaching is an art — an art so great and so difficult to master that a man or a woman can spend a long life at it, without realizing much more than his limitations and his mistakes and his distance from the ideal. But the main aim of my happy days has been to become a good teacher, just as every architect wishes to be a good architect, and every professional poet strives toward perfection."

ILLINOIS DAY - GOVERNOR'S DAY
MOOSEHEART,
June 11

WHEN I CAME HERE A long time ago to see this famous place and look at all the Moose and their works, it never occurred to me that I might some day be standing in this exposed position with all the Moose looking at me. Being initiated into a fraternal order is a new experience for me, but the courtesy and cordiality you have shown me today have been so heart warming, the visible evidence of the great humanitarian work being done here is so impressive, I realize that I've missed something very rewarding. I suspect that the other members of this large new class of initiates feel the same way.

I am being recognized and honored here today in this signal way because, for better or for worse, I am the Governor of Illinois. Yet I am well aware that in the activities of the Loyal Order of Moose it is men that count, and not titles. I have been assured that in this order all members are accorded the same rights and privileges, the same recognition in the eyes of their fellow members. Each contributes to the strength of the society and each shares equally in its benefits. Certainly everything I have seen and heard about the Moose order supports those proud claims. And certainly we have evidence of this equality of opportunity and of benevolence here at Mooseheart.

The members of this order come from every walk of life, from every economic stratum, and from diverse national origins. Neither their religious beliefs nor their political affliliations are conditions of membership and participation in the work. There are no class distinctions to divide them. In this sort of fraternity men can not only find fellowship but give expression to their broadest ideals and loyalties as American citizens.

The age in which we live is one of strange contradictions. The first half of the twentieth century has produced many moral, social and scientific advances; at the same time it was producing a great depression and two world wars that have established it as the bloodiest half century in the whole Christian era.

It may well be that when the definitive history of this century is finally written it will record as the most significant development of its first fifty years, not the two world wars or the depression, not the Russian revolution or the rise and fall of Hitler, not even the atom bomb, but rather the expansion of the intellectual and moral horizons of millions of people.

That expansion has been evidenced in America by two striking developments: first, the recognition of our responsibility as a nation in the world community, and second, a deeper appreciation of our individual and collective responsibility to alleviate human suffering — a growing concern for human well-being.

What has happened here at Mooseheart is but one evidence of this quickened social conscience. There are many other evidences, both in government and in the charitable activities of many other private agencies. It is reflected in the development of the fraternal benefit associations, in the evolution of the workmen's compensation and unemployment insurance laws, the old age pension system and more recently in increased retirement security for industrial workers through private pension plans. The broadening of educational opportunities for more people is another evidence.

We cannot know what the next half-century has in store for us, but if we could somehow carry to the rest of the world the lesson in fraternity that this order teaches, we do know it would be a happier era for all mankind. We could set at rest anxiety and fear, and channel into the constructive pursuits of peace the energies and resources we now apply in self defense to the creation of new instruments of destruction. If we could impart to others this spirit of human brotherhood which has enriched our lives, we might at last banish forever the ancient curse of self-destruction that has plagued mankind since the beginning of time.

Even now, this and a number of other fraternal orders are international in scope and their outposts are being extended constantly. Thus their combined influence can help to strengthen the machinery for peace which is being built slowly, painfully, pray God surely. Thus they may help to bring nearer the ancient everlasting vision of world peace.

Disappointments and frustrations must not divert us from that goal. We must keep on translating good will into action, as has been done here, to make our world a better place in the things of the spirit as well as in material things. Therein lies our best hope — indeed our only hope — for bringing reality to the golden promises of our century.

76

DEDICATION OF MEMORIAL HOSPITAL FAIRFIELD
June 25

T HE PROBLEM OF MAKING good medical care available to all who need it is going to be one of the big social questions before the American people in the next few years. It is recognized that the problem is national in scope; various bills dealing with it in one way or another are pending in the Congress even now. It is a problem that calls for our best thought. I doubt if it can be solved quickly. I know it cannot be solved by epithets and political demagoguery. The ultimate solution may be far away, and it may lie in some compromise between private initiative and government initiative, or both — even as you have done here in Fairfield.

Underlying all of the arguments are important intangibles, not the least of which is how far the power of government should be extended. What are the limits of government's responsibility for the individual? When does welfare become tyranny? These are questions which the American people still have the power to decide and which, pray God, they always will have.

Some cynics say we are not what we like to think we are —individuals capable of making intelligent decisions regarding our own affairs. I am not among those who hold such a view. I believe that in ninety-nine cases out of a hundred, the American people will make the right decision — if and when they are in possession of the essential facts about any given issue. It's a big "if" and a long "when". The problem is how to get the facts to them — the actual facts, not what someone says the facts are to serve some personal or political end. I wish you could see my mail — the things, foolish and important, that people blame me for which I didn't do, or couldn't do, or never heard of. Yes, and the people who, only occasionally, thank me for things I didn't do.

Public information — keeping busy people honestly and accurately informed — is a public administrator's most difficult job, and ignorance or public misinformation his biggest obstacle. I am reminded of it every day when someone misbrands rumor or falsehood as fact and it is picked up and repeated as fact. Someone once said that a falsehood will travel round the world while truth is pulling on its boots.

But somehow truth usually wins the day, and it's a healthy thing that people are thinking and talking about adequate medical care for the rich and poor alike. In a democracy, such widespread debate and discussion is the first step toward the affirmative action that ultimately solves the people's problems.

Speaking of medical care reminds me that we talk much of heart disease, of cancer, of tuberculosis and the afflictions of man, but we talk all too little of the greatest affliction of all, the plague of our time on earth —worry and fear. I said last Sunday at the University of Illinois Commencement that this was the Anxious Age; that we were moved more by anxiety and fear than by hope and faith; that we are doubting our beliefs and believing our doubts. We worry about keeping our jobs — even we politicians! We worry about security for our old age, about the future, about war; we even worry about peace and what it would do to prices and prosperity. Fear that assails the mind and spirit can be as dangerous as infections that assail the body. We become ill because we're worried. Then we get more worried because we're ill. And finally there we are — calling the doctor and knocking at the hospital door.

On this fine Sunday afternoon while we are dedicating this fine hospital to health and hope it might be well to remember that Jesus has been called the Great Physician. Maybe we could add the Great Psychiatrist, for this is what he said: "Come unto me and I will give you rest." "Be not anxious for the morrow; for the morrow will be anxious for itself. Sufficient unto the day is the evil thereof."

Now, my friends of Fairfield, that may not be a solution of the medical assistance problem, but I think you will all agree that a little less fear and frenzy, and a little more of the Great Physician's prescription of faith and serenity would certainly reduce the patient population in this splendid new hospital — which I am proud to dedicate and for which I both commend and thank a proud and enterprising community of Illinois.

150TH ANNIVERSARY OF THE ORGANIZATION OF THE INDIANA TERRITORY, VINCENNES, INDIANA
July 4

As THE GOVERNOR OF ILLINOIS I am much honored to be invited to pay this neighborly visit to Vincennes for the celebration of the Sesquicentennial of the Indiana Territory. And it didn't take much urging on the part of my good friend, Governor Schricker, and Judge Shake to get me over here. I wanted to come because of the historical significance of this anniversary, not only to Indiana but to Illinois as well, and also because it seemed to me most fitting that it should be celebrated in this honored and venerable city where our Western history dawned in bloodshed, romance and chivalry. I bring to you and all of the people of Indiana the greetings and congratulations of the eight million citizens of Illinois — and the thanks of all those who are proud of our past, the prelude of our future.

As a matter of fact, we in Illinois would have felt a little offended if you hadn't invited us to this birthday party. We look upon this as a family affair and we are proud to be a member of the Indiana family — and no black sheep either. As all of you here in Vincennes well know, most of what is now the State of Illinois was once a part of the Indiana Territory. Fort St. Louis, LaSalle's stronghold at Starved Rock, is gone. So are Creve Coeur, Kaskaskia and Fort Chartres. Little remains of the first coming of the white man down the rivers and across the prairies but the little village of Cahokia on the Mississippi and imperishable Vincennes on the Wabash.

Founded first about 1700 as a French trading post in an Indian village, Vincennes passed to the British in the French and Indian War in 1763, and then to the immortal George Rogers Clark in a historic battle known to every American school boy. Nor do I forget that his dauntless soldiers came not from the eastern battlefields of the Revolution but from the west across the whole breadth of Illinois.

Once capital of the Northwest Territory, briefly capital of the Louisiana Purchase, Vincennes became the capital of the Indiana Territory, the largest American territory ever governed from a territorial capital.

From 1800 to 1809 Vincennes was our capital as it was yours. Our forebears fought the Indians together; they hunted, trapped and fished together, and I suppose tried to get the best of each other in a few business deals. Of course I don't know whether shrewd Hoosier business deals had anything to do with it. But at any rate, it wasn't long before we Illinoisans decided to go it alone and set up our own territory. We acquired a governor of our own and set him up in business in Kaskaskia. But please understand that while we separated, history does not record that Indiana filed a bill for divorce against Illinois, nor sought to disinherit us!

Indiana beat us into the Union by two years — you joined in 1816 and we in 1818 — but we have grown up fast and developed some big muscles too. I know that we should show proper deference to our elders, so I will resist the temptation to do a little selling on Illinois.

Through the years there has been a close kinship between us. We have been friendly rivals in everything from corn and hog farming to football and politics; but we also have been good neighbors with few squabbles to mar a happy relationship.

Indiana's past is peculiarly its own, but in its larger outlines the history of this state is the history of Illinois and the other states that make up the great region we call the middle west. Here were epitomized the two great forces that built the nation — migration and westward movement — where Europeans first became Americans in reality rather than Europeans transplanted. Here were symbol and reality — rivers, forests, prairies, of plain people, neighborliness and democracy — all symbols of the American dream. Here is the heartland; here is big business and little business; cities and villages, factories and farms; here industry and agriculture balance. This is the heartland — but you'll forgive me if I feel obliged to remind you that the center of population of the United States recently crossed the Wabash into an adjoining state of Illinois!

And here too is the cradle of mid-western American manners and morals, folkways and customs, religion and politics. From here too has come that train of social and economic problems which follow in the wake of a complex industrial society built upon the foundation of an agrarian economy. The story of our progress is the story of how those problems have been met and will be met through energies, skills and wisdom of a free people.

Indiana, and my own state of Illinois, are fine examples of that robust regionalism which characterizes the middle west. America is a community of regions, each contributing to the national structure. But perhaps no other section has clung as tenaciously to its regional identity as the middle west, even though its people sprang from diverse origins. New Englanders and Southerners were numerous among the Indiana pioneers; Frenchmen, Englishmen, Germans and Swedes and Norwegians there were too, drawn by the rich promise of the new land and loving its prairies like they loved the mountains of their homelands. And everywhere there was the tempo of the frontier and the pattern of the pioneer, strong builders, sturdy fighters, adventurous explorers, courageous men striving for something better, with dignity and pride. Here men of all ranks and origins were merged into middle-western Americans, from which flowed other men and resources and other forces to perpetuate the solid union which comes through the unity of diversities.

Julia Henderson Levering in her penetrating account of Indiana's past *Historic Indiana* had this to say of the quality of the people here in the midland of America:

> There is in the middle west a social temper which seeks the best in things of the mind and of the spirit. We have fallen heir —legitimately enough — to the idealism of the New Englander. Perhaps the twin spirits of idealism and shrewd utilitarianism

which were pretty clearly to be distinguished in our Yankee forebears have fused in some degree in us, so that at one angle we seem to have lost one, and at another angle the other. Yet they both remain, modified but active, and the result is a social life in reality finer, stronger, more wholesome, at least more vitalized, one may say without offense, than in any other region.

Nowhere in America are ideas more welcome. Nowhere are they examined with more self-control. We are the most teachable of communities and we are, beneath everything, the most aspiring. If we are naive, if we lack urbanity, finish, it is because we are fresh, exuberant, and quite young. But those who come to know the life of the West come to realize that its humanity is large and deep, and that its grave and kindly spirit will bear us far. The quality of moral and intellectual earnestness that is the main current of the life of our region, is pretty generally underestimated. Yet it is the factor, one believes, of greatest importance in the life of America today. It is well for the West to recognize this, not boastfully, but with a sense of all it involves.

ADDRESS TO 33rd DIVISION NATIONAL GUARD CAMP McCOY, WISCONSIN
July 9

THE EVENTS OF RECENT days in Korea are so ominous to every American, and of such potential concern to every member of the National Guard, that they command our first concern and give added meaning to the program of training which your units have been undergoing here. Everyone hopes — and there are some heartening indications — that the fighting in Korea will be local and not the fuse of a third and greater holocaust.

But the cold, hard fact is that less than six years after the end of World War II Americans have been compelled to take up arms again. And the Congress of the United States, with overwelming unanimity of judgment on the part of members of all parties, has enacted the draft extension bill which authorized the President to mobilize the organized reserves and the National Guard to active duty whenever it is deemed necessary. That bill passed the United States Senate 76 to 0; it passed the House of Representatives 315 to 4. That almost unanimous vote in both houses can only reflect the unity of sentiment among our people.

No one likes the idea of drafting young men into the armed forces. No one likes the idea of compelling men to sacrifice years of their lives to war. We hope and fervently pray that it will not be necessary to draft young men or call up the Reserves and the National Guard, but we know that the draft law was essential for the security of our country and the safety of our people.

As soldiers, you know better than the average citizen the meaning of war. You know the misery and the suffering and horror of it. But you also know that we must do more than hope for peace. We must back up our hopes and prayers and words with the only kind of strength a military aggressor can understand. And we must prove to the world that we will fight for peace if we have to. We want no more Munichs. We know from sad and bloody experience that appeasement begets more appeasement and finally disaster. We know that the *strong* can't avoid being the *responsible* as well. So we have drawn the sword in unprecedented resistance to cynical, brutal, shameless aggression.

We could do no less. Through the United Nations more than forty nations have raised a chorus of protest and denunciation, and we may be sure that Russia understands the determination of the free world better now than she did a month ago. There must be as few weak spots as possible to tempt Soviet penetration. Whether the men in the Kremlin thought they could unify Korea without resistance, or whether they merely were using Korea as a test of our determination to meet the challenge of communist expansion elsewhere in the world, they have the answer now.

And it is not the answer of the President, or of the Congress or of the United Nations, or of governments alone. It is the answer of free people everywhere who have had enough. It is the answer of the American people who, as in every clear-cut national emergency, stand unitedly together. We cannot know what the eventual outcome of this tragedy will be, but we do know it has lighted a flame of indignation in the hearts of peaceful, decent men and women throughout the world. And that indignation —the evidence that the free nations will stand together to meet the challenge — is the best hope we have for peace on earth. For a vigilant world must sometimes convince the Soviet Union that it cannot accomplish its design by penetration and domination; and an outraged world must convince them now that they cannot win by force.

Perhaps there is a morsel of comfort for us in this ugly hour in Shakespeare's words (Henry V, Act IV, Scene I)

There is some soul of goodness in things evil,
Would men observingly distil it out;
For our bad neighbour makes us early stirrers
Which is both healthful and good husbandry.
Besides, they are our outward consciences,
And preachers to us all; admonishing
That we should dress us fairly for our end.
Thus may we gather honey from the weed,
And make a moral of the devil himself.

CENTENNIAL CELEBRATION, ST. ANNE
July 28

I AM DELIGHTED THAT I could come to your centennial festival and have this small part in it. I have throughly enjoyed this afternoon's colorful parade. You have done a fine job of re-creating some of the atmosphere and the semblance of the St. Anne that your fathers and grandfathers knew in pioneer days.

I am happy to bring to the people of St. Anne the felicitations and the congratulations of the State of Illinois on this notable anniversary. I know you are proud that St. Anne has reached this milestone that establishes it as one of the oldest municipalities in Illinois.

You here in St. Anne have managed to achieve in a marked degree a happy balance between the old and the new in your community life. You have retained through the years many of the traditions and the spirit —even some of the customs — of the French-Canadian settlers who came to this site a hundred years ago, and many of whose descendents live today in this attractive, proud community.

Your centennial celebration displays the kind of civic spirit which explains why this community has retained its unique character through the years and why you at the same time kept pace with that nebulous thing we call progress.

"Progress" suggests the antithesis. Sometime ago I drove over a part of Route 1 in this vicinity. State Route 1 was one of the very first highways to be paved when Illinois began its ambitious program of concrete highway building some thirty years ago. As you all know, Route 1 roughly follows the old Hubbard Trail, so named because it was marked off in the 1820's by the wagon wheels of the fur-trader Gurdon S. Hubbard traveling the route between Fort Dearborn and Vincennes. It is a route linked closely to the early development of Illinois; as such it always has occupied a high place among the historic arteries of travel within our borders.

After driving over Route 1, I can better understand why it is that the people of St. Anne and of this section of Illinois have been clamoring so loudly to Springfield — and why Representative Sam Shapiro has been camping on my doorstep —insisting that something be done to retrieve this highway from its present state of deterioration. I'll quickly concede that it is in a deplorable condition, and something must be done about it. But many other highways in Illinois are in little if any better condition and something should and must be done about them too.

We think of a century as a long time, but in the perspective of history it is but a moment. We think of this as an old community, but almost two centuries before it took form the first white men were coming down the rivers and across the prairies of Illinois, to explore, to bring the word of God to the Indian tribes, and to barter with them for furs.

Long before Father Charles Chiniquy came to this site from Bourbonnais, accompanied by most of his French-Canadian parishioners, the history of Illinois was being shaped in the 1670's and 1680's by the explorations of Father Marquette and Louis Jolliet and LaSalle and those who came after them. It was they who brought to the new land the influences — religious, commerical and cultural — of the French people.

That influence was great in the formative years of the Illinois territory and in Illinois' early statehood. It has continued through the years to contribute to the heterogeneous character of our Illinois citizenry. It remains today in many of our place names, in our genealogy and in the culture of our people.

It was the French, in the early decades of the 18th Century, bound together by their race and the common purpose of subduing the wilderness, who first achieved the rough outlines of a unified society here in the midwest. "Under the utmost difficulties," wrote a Jesuit priest, "we are striving to bring order to this wilderness."

The French settlements that were scattered about the Illinois country followed many of the patterns of the Old World. The church was the center of social as well as religious activity, as was the case here in St. Anne. And the church ranked in importance and influence with the civil authority. A portion of the land was designated for common fields, and for mutual protection from the Indians, agricultural workers went out to their narrow strips of soil each day together and returned to the village each night.

But the British conquered the French and the period of chaos that followed was ended with the American conquest. As the frontier moved westward settlers of every nationality began pouring into Illinois. Gone now are Fort St. Louis, LaSalle's stronghold at Starved Rock. Gone too are Creve Coeur, Kaskaskia and Fort Chartres. But there remain today as echoes of the French period, towns like Cahokia and Vincennes and St. Anne and many others whose names and the names of whose people already reflect their origin and their cultural descent from the honored and earliest of our pioneers, the French.

I hope that the people of St. Anne will cling to their proud traditions and that the passage of time will bring no waning of your civic consciousness and courage. Our whole national structure is built on a foundation of small communities. Our national interest requires that they retain a strong spirit of self-reliance and self-betterment, which will preserve their vitality and their individuality.

It is in the small towns that we most often find the richest values of community life — the neighborliness, the understanding, the common interest and the mutual help. At the same time the disadvantages of small communities — limited economic and social opportunity and prejudice —have had an increasing tendency in recent years to drive many of the more vigorous and enterprising young people away. It behooves the leaders of the small towns to do everything they can to check that trend. One of the ways to do this is to make young people keenly aware of the spiritual rewards, the fundamental values of community living, the many compensations of small town life in this area of urban concentrations, to make them understand, if you please, that "the good life" is where you make it.

Our cherished liberties are being challenged again today in the bloody arena of armed conflict. We have been compelled again to draw the sword against ruthless aggression, to prove again that we will fight to keep the freedom which has been handed down to us, the freedom that has made America a shining symbol of opportunity and individual achievement.

Thus, as we cast a backward glance at the past, our eyes naturally turn to the struggle in which we are engaged and to what the future holds. I think this community celebration —which is one of many similar historical fetes that have been held in other communities of the middle west this summer — is but a reflection of our unity and our will to preserve the mode of life that exists here in St. Anne, and in all of the other St. Anne's throughout the length and breadth of our land.

The building of this community, like the building of America, entailed a long and hard struggle. Destiny has given to this generation another long and hard and bloody struggle to save what our forbears have wrought and to forge a structure for peace which will blot out the evil shadow of tyranny creeping across the earth and let us live in a world where no one rattles a sword and no one drags a chain.

That day may be, and probably is, farther away than we like to think. But we must face up to our obligations, in concert with the more than fifty other nations who have sided with us in the determination to stand fast once more while still we may. We must carry on the struggle, costly as it may be, with the same faith, and courage and resolution which enabled those earlier Americans to overcome the obstacles they faced.Only by doing so can we be true to ourselves and our past; only by so doing can we hope to make our past a prelude to a happier, more glorious future.

NAUVOO STATE PARK
September 9

THE PAST SPEAKS TO US of many things, and, if we will but listen, there is much to be learned, much by which to be comforted in time of present peril. Those voices are quite audible here in Nauvoo. For one thing, I think of the many peoples and faiths which have existed in this place. Starting as an Indian village, it has housed a unique procession of pioneer settlers which included such contrasting groups as the Mormons and Icarians, who sought this haven to pursue their own beliefs about the nature of man and the proper organization of society, and the Germans who fled Europe in the dread year of 1848 seeking only the most basic of political and civil liberties.

There is much to be learned from all this as to the virtues of tolerence in such things as religious beliefs, and I suggest to you that the ease with which your community today accomodates varying faiths is a wholesome product of this history. This has been in my mind as I have gone about today observing your community with its different churches and the magnificent site of the new building of the Benedictine Sisters which is soon to rise in your midst.

The bounty of grapes which you celebrate today flows from roots brought here from abroad and by an alien people. Your famous blue cheese is an art imported from abroad. They are a vivid reminder of the melting-pot which is America. In our variety has been —and is — our strength. What like contributions to our future welfare may not be made by the displaced persons of our generation if we will only heed this mute but eloquent message whispering all about us here today!

I would suggest also to you the magnitude of our debt to the past in terms of maturing political wisdom. The Icarians—those gentle communists of a vanished time — have provided us with a living proof that a free society is the best society, that in the untrammeled interplay of individual initiative and competition there is the greatest hope for material progress and spiritual serenity. These forebears here escaped the degradation of the police state in the pursuit of their political and economic Utopia, but they learned, to their sorrow and for our everlasting instruction, that there are basic values which must go by the board in any such effort to cast the incentives and aspirations of human beings in a mold of that character.

Their example speaks to us loudly across the years, and here on the prairies of the Middle West we are correspondingly better capable of understanding the division presently confronting mankind. Confident of the rightness of our cause, and aware of the consequences of defeat, we can face the sacrifices we will be called upon to make with a greater fortitude and a determination more grim.

It is now one hundred years since many of the residents of old Nauvoo first came to live on the banks of the Great River. Many of them, notably the French and Germans, were fleeing the cruel repressions with which the reactionary ruling governments of the day in Europe had throttled the many libertarian movements of 1848. The shocking fate of these efforts were fresh in memory and charged with despair for further attempts. And the more perceptive of the victims who had abandoned hope for the Old World and sought refuge in the New, found a growing rift in the political and social structure of this new homeland which could only end, as it did, in a bitter and bloody war — one which seemed likely to destroy the new republic and to dim its bright light of promise and hope for believers in freedom everywhere.

It was hardly a time for optimism or for assuming that the promised land had been reached. The horizons of America were darkly edged and its future full of sorrowful calamity. But courageous men, including an honorable representation of these same immigrants, pushed on to face up to the issue of human freedom as it was presented a century ago, and to win an eventual triumph.

In 1950 there are causes of despair similar to those of 1850. The age-old and seemingly endless struggle against the enslavement of one man by another is breaking out again, only this time it is in a breath-takingly wider arena. We of this day have the remembered agony of two terrible wars in defense of freedom in our lifetime, and now the chilling awareness that the familiar pattern of conquest has reappeared in more fearsome form than ever before.

There is much in the present to make us disheartened, but the circumstances in which we are now meeting remind us that there is also much in the past to give us courage, and hope, and strength. The panorama of history which has unfolded here at Nauvoo is full of promise for the future because it is studded with demonstrations of the unlimited capacities of the human spirit to remain unyielding in the darkest of adversities and boldly to pluck the flower of safety from the nettle of danger.

As those who have gone before won through in their time against the perennial enemy, so shall we in ours. But how encouraging it is to have in these critical days the concrete knowledge of their struggle and their success. And how fortunate we are to have about us here these visible reminders that men and women have large resources of heart and mind for shaping their fate and for leaving marks of their being which, to the pleasure and profit of succeeding generations, resist the relentless surge of time.

I congratulate you of Nauvoo for your beautiful festival of wine and cheese and for the fight you have successfully waged to preserve this heritage. I express to you the thanks of the people of Illinois for the benefits you have brought to them by this work. And, with the dedication of Nauvoo State Park, I join their efforts to yours for the greater good of the State of Illinois — now and hereafter.

CHICAGO HISTORICAL SOCIETY GETTYSBURG ADDRESS EXHIBIT
November 19

LINCOLN'S ADDRESS AT GETTYSBURG four score and seven years ago has special meaning today. For it was a plea to Americans to reaffirm their faith in democracy. Then, as now, democracy was sorely threatened. Then, as now, American boys were pouring out their life blood to preserve democracy. Then, as now, while some gave "the last full measure of devotion," others complained that the burden was too crushing.

Lincoln had a broad conception of the Civil War. He saw it in global dimensions. It was not only the American Union that was imperiled. Upon the fate of the Union hung the fate of the world democracy.

In Lincoln's time the United States was the only major country of the world that enjoyed the democratic form of government, the only land where government was of, by, and for the people. Elsewhere, emperors or kings or oligarchies controlled, often exploiting the common man. Our government was unique and still regarded as an experiment. America was democracy's proving ground. The masses of other lands looked to us with hope: if our experiment proved successful, they too might win self-government. But the privileged groups, regarding our democratic experiment with foreboding, identified it with mob rule and lawlessness, sneered and prophesied its doom. When civil war threatened the disruption of the United States, the enemies of democracy were smugly pleased. They could cry, "We told you so," as government of the people seemed about to prove a false hope.

But Lincoln resolved that government of the people must not fail. The mission of America was to demonstrate its superiority. Lincoln was a man of peace. A brothers' war seemed frightful to him. Yet he realized that what America stood for was worth bloodshed and sacrifice.

As Lincoln saw the issue, the Confederate states had rejected two fundamental precepts of democracy. First, in refusing to accept him as their President and making his election their justification for withdrawing from the Union, they had violated the first rule of democratic government, the obligation of a minority to abide by a result of an election. Without such acquiescence democracy would not work. The Union must never be dissevered for any such reason as this. It is for essentially the same reason that we are fighting in Korea under the United Nations banner today.

Second, in making slavery the foundation stone of their new government, the Confederates were renouncing the doctrine of the equal rights of man in favor of the creed of the master race, an idea that Lincoln abhorred. "The last, best hope of earth," in his view, was to be found in those precepts of our Declaration of Independence which affirmed that all men are created equal, that they are endowed by their Creator with certain inalienable rights, among which are life, liberty and the pursuit of happiness.

Here, in fact, was the whole pith and substance of Lincoln's political philosophy. Here, in his deep reverence for the rights of man as proclaimed in our American charter of freedom, is to be found the explanation of most of his political actions." I have never had a feeling politically," he said, "which did not spring from the sentiments embodied in the Declaration of Independence." It was these principles, Lincoln believed, that would lift artificial weights from men's shoulders, clear the paths of laudable pursuit for all, and afford all an unfettered start and a fair chance in the race of life.

When we realize that Lincoln saw the threatened disruption of the Union as a threat to democratic government throughout the world, his words at Gettysburg became more meaningful. Chancellorsville, Antietam, Chickamauga and Gettysburg were deciding more than the fate of these United States. American boys were dying for all people everywhere.

So when Lincoln was asked to speak at the dedication of the national cemetery at Gettysburg, he welcomed the chance to tell the people what those three days of bloody battle meant and to explain what those men died for, as he saw it.

His thoughts went back four score and seven years to the revolutionary founding of this nation, conceived in liberty and dedicated to the proposition that all men are created equal. Then his mind came back to the war being fought to determine whether that nation, or any nation conceived in revolution and dedicated to such radical principles, could long endure—whether the people were capable of shaping their own destiny. He thought of the heroic dead, and of what the living owed them for their sacrifice. Mere words were inadequate to express it. The world, he thought, would little note nor long remember what was said that day. Then Lincoln looked ahead —not merely to the tomorrow, but into the far distant future, as he said: "It is for us, the living, rather to be here dedicated to the great task remaining before us — that from these honored dead we take increased devotion to that task for which they gave the last full measure of devotion, that we here highly resolve that these dead shall not have died in vain; that this nation, under God, shall have a new birth of freedom; and that government of the people, by the people, for the people, shall not perish from the earth."

The war ended. The nation reunited, once again offered hope for liberal yearnings everywhere. Inspired by the example of America, democracy made striking headway throughout the world, even among the so-called backward people of the earth. It seemed that the principles for which Lincoln fought and died would win world-wide acceptance. The people of America took this for granted. To us it became merely a question of when and how. America became complaisant. She lost sight of her mission. Too often, she took a selfish, limited view, ignoring the struggle of other people to shape their own affairs and win more of life's blessings for themselves.

Then came the shock of World War I. But with victory, democracy took up its march again. Russia, most reactionary of all European countries, set up a people's government. Germany, Austria, Czechoslovakia, became republics. Woodrow Wilson, who saw the fate of democracy as the prime issue of the war, went to Europe with a purpose to mark out new boundaries which would express, as nearly as possible, the people's will. Democracy was again in the ascendant. And America shrouded herself in isolation.

The rest is within the recollection of us all. Adolph Hitler resurrected the malevolent doctrine of the master race, and poised its ghastly death's-head over Europe. And now comes Russian Communism, threatening political thralldom through enslavement of men's minds, stalking democracy throughout the world.

The struggle for human liberty goes on. It must be re-fought by every generation, for democracy is threatened not alone by foreign ideologies, but by selfishness, indifference, intolerance, demagoguery and disloyalty to public trust right here at home. Lincoln's fight is not finished. The far future into which he looked is here, and we are now the living. Four score and seven years after he uttered these immortal words, it is for us to be re-dedicated to our democratic faith. It is now for us, the living to be here dedicated to the great task, the same task, remaining before us.

1951

DEDICATION OF ALL-FAITH CHAPEL, TRAINING SCHOOL FOR BOYS, ST. CHARLES
May 6

M Y PURPOSE HERE IS TO express the gratitude of the state administration for the helpful interest which you of St. Charles and the Fox River Valley have taken in the management of this training school, and particularly in the building of this simple but impressive chapel which we hope will, in future years, give increasing emphasis to the spiritual phase of the educational program being carried on here.

St. Charles nowadays is a great experiment. Many are cynical and skeptical. For the accent here is upon growth, development and achievement rather than upon discipline and punishment. Here we recognize that it is more important to teach right from wrong than the three R's. Here the emphasis is upon spiritual as well as academic education. I think it is agreed by almost everyone that education which does not take into account religion is deficient and negligent in one of the great areas of human experience. Education and religion are natural allies. Especially is this true, it seems to me, in an institution like this which has a special problem in training boys who frequently have been deprived of the religious contacts and encouragement they would receive in a normal home environment.

So I am delighted that this chapel has come to pass, to provide the boys who come here for a portion of their lives with a place where they may worship in the manner of their choice, and in the atmosphere of reverence which should surround every place of worship.

This is not a penal institution. It is an institution wherein we seek to train and rehabilitate boys whom the law classifies as delinquents. The philosophy of this institution is that every boy who is sent here is an individual with a mind, a body and a soul — an individual with his own hopes, fears and longings, with his own individual personality and problems.

These boys are here for many reasons. It is easy to say that they are here because they are law violators, that they are misdemeanants, or young criminals deserving punishment more than sympathy. But all of us know that the fault is not theirs alone. We know that in some instances, perhaps many, society itself must assume part of the blame for their presence here. We must assume part of the responsibility for the short-comings of environment, for the bad housing and the slum conditions in some of our cities, for the poor schools and for the poverty and social degradation which is all that some of these boys have known.No one can say how many of these boys would not be here except for reasons of economic insecurity, lack of parental interest, and worse, over which they had no control.

Many say that society devotes too little time and effort, and too little money, to the correction of the conditions which breed crime. This is a large subject, and certainly one to which the people of America would do well to give more thought. Certainly some strong arguments can be advanced in support of the contention that our sense of values is weirdly out of focus when we spend one hundred billion dollars a year for our physical necessities while total contributions for our churches average only $320 millions a year; when each year the American people spend four times as much on amusements as they do in gifts to educational institu-tions. And, it is a tragic circumstance of our time that we must spend seventy per cent of our national budget for defense and for destruction, and less than a third of the national budget for all of the functions of government and the constructive things which would bring more of the benefits and advantages of our advanced technology to more of our peo-ple. So we work toward and pray for the day when the vast expenditures of war can be diverted to mankind's progress.

The very fact that this is an All-Faith chapel, and that there were held here this morning services for Protestant, Catholic and Jewish boys, sym-bolizes the religious freedom, the tolerance and the brotherhood which is the essence of all religions and the foundation of our hopes for better world understanding. We have here an object lesson in tolerance, a con-crete evidence of the spirit of brotherhood which must be an essential part of a truly Christian educational process.

After all, democracy is nothing more than an attempt to apply Christian principles to a human society. Our forefathers came together in a com-mon faith in one God. They printed on their money —"In God We Trust. Then they said to each other in effect: "Under this faith we do not need a king, or a dictator, or an over-all ruler, because we respect each other and we value other's individuality, personality and freedom. Furthermore, we are determined that the rights of each individual to life, liberty, and the pursuit of happiness, are the responsiblities of all individuals to maintain and further."

Some say we have lost, at least in part, this basic concept of democracy. But I do not believe this. I believe that while the strength of our religious convictions and our faith is not as great as we would like, or as universal, it nevertheless remains strong among us and stands today as one of the greatest of our weapons of defense against aggression.

The Western world cannot thwart Communism by being afraid of it, or by being angry at it. We can win only by having a better answer. That better answer lies in the simplest principles of Christianity expressed in the real terms of hope and opportunity of every individual to have identity, individuality, respect, and a share of the good things in life.

No one knows, unless it be the men in the Kremlin, whether we may have to fight another war for the survival of government by the consent of the governed. But victory must come, sooner or later, because Communism is more a conspiracy than a people. It exploits want and deprivation among great masses of the world. And I should think victory over Communism can be won without the holocaust of another war if we succeed in two things: if we free men are able to make ourselves so strong that the Kremlin will be convinced that the race is lost, and if we are able, while doing this, to make enough of the underprivileged peoples of the world understand that Communism is nothing more than a conspiracy, a cruel, false hope for improvement of their way of life. Our task, perhaps the most difficult we ever have faced, is to make the miserable, uncommitted millions of the earth see that the alternative is not more bread, but the lash, the chains of slavery, and the end of hope for individual dignity.

One of the ways, perhaps the only way, we can bring these truths to the world is by example. We can only demonstrate what democracy is by how it works. Let me cite one illustration.

On the grounds of this institution is a building known as Horner Hall, so called in honor of one of my illustrious predecessors, Governor Henry Horner. Illinois remembers him with affection and admiration, and I think his career will always be an example of the hope and opportunity for many in this free land.

Before me Illinois has had but three governors of my political party — in the ninety years since the Civil War. The first was John Peter Altgeld — the Eagle Forgotten — a German immigrant; the second was Edward F. Dunne, only one generation removed from Ireland; the third was Henry Horner, son of an immigrant. John Peter Altgeld was a Protestant, Edward F. Dunne was a Catholic, and Henry Horner was a Jew.

That is the American story. It is the dream which democracy has made real here in America, on the prairies of Illinois. And it illustrates how our way of life — the way of tolerence and brotherhood — has enabled us to learn to live together and largely overcome the age-old antagonisms and rivalries which our earliest settlers brought with them to this country. It is the lesson we hope the world will somehow, sometime learn.

This is a dream we must keep bright among our own people, here in this institution and everywhere — hope and opportunity for all —boys, men and nations who are steadfast enough to earn and keep their freedom.

VETERANS MENTAL HOSPITAL DAY, DANVILLE
May 20

I REALLY DIDN'T COME HERE today to make a speech. I came here today primarily to visit this famous hospital and to pay tribute to all those individuals and organizations in the Danville community who join together each year to sponsor this program. I think it is admirable indeed that your civic and service clubs and veterans' organizations should arrange this Hospital Day, encouraging the people of the community to visit this splendid institution and to interest themselves in what is being done here to restore to active, useful lives thousands of men who have suffered so cruelly from the barbarity of war.

I am aware that this is not a one-day enterprise — that throughout the year you carry on a varied program of recreation and entertainment for the patients. By what you are doing, above and beyond the activities of the hospital itself, you are helping to bring an added measure of happiness into the daily lives of these men. You are helping to speed the rehabilitation of those for whom cure is possible, and you are brightening the path of those for whom there is no cure.

It would be easy for all of you who devote your precious time and energy to this work to say: this is not our obligation; this is a government hospital — let the government worry about it. It would be easy to say that you have no responsiblity for these patients merely because this hospital happens to be located in Danville.

But your community has not followed this easy course; you have not passed on the other side of the street like the Levite in the Biblical story of the Good Samaritan. You have discharged an added obligation to these men who bore arms that all of us might live in freedom, an obligation that no act of Congress, no appropriation of public funds, no government assistance could possibly discharge.

You visit the sick and so I commend and congratulate you for your enterprise and your charity. I believe that if this program could be emulated in every community in America, our people who are still almost untouched by war would become more conscious of its ugly realities and what it really means. They would come to understand war not just in terms of today's taxes and today's casualty lists, in terms of inconvenience, disruptions in family life, and temporary economic disarrangements, but in terms of the pain and suffering and mental anguish in the long tomorrow.

If every citizen of Illinois could, for example, be taken on a tour of this hospital, or any of the large veterans' hospitals for that matter, it would be a far more persuasive argument for the United Nations, for collective security, for every device of force and of law to forbid and prevent war than a million of the most eloquent words ever written or spoken.

We see here at this great hospital what war can do to the minds of men. We see here one of its cruelest legacies. Undergoing treatment here are hundreds of men, who, except for their experiences in combat, would be leading normal happy lives today. Happily, many of them completely recover. But I think that no one could visit this largest of the government mental hospitals, and the rapidly growing number of other veterans hospitals, without realizing that the ultimate abolition of war is the most important unfinished business of the human race. Cynicism and defeatism about the war against war is neither worldly nor wise; it is primitive and stupid.

Right now the abolition of war seems a more elusive and distant prospect than at any time in our sanguinary past. But the hope for the future lies in the present. There was never a better time than now for the American people to be giving soul-searching thought to how today's decisions and actions may affect the course of history, how those decisions and actions may speed or delay the day when war will be an outmoded instrument for settling international disputes.

During the last few weeks the American people have been stirred as they seldom have before by the great debate over the course of our foreign policy. People everywhere — in Congress, in our homes, in our schools, in the market places, on every street corner — are asking themselves: what lies ahead, peace or war? More peace or more war?

The great controversy of the moment centers around our immediate military course in Korea. Should we expand our military operations in Asia or try to localize them? Which is the surer path to peace? People ask each other: "Are you for MacArthur or Truman?"

But I submit that question is beside the point. The point is not who is right, but what is right. I think the controversy which rages has been too much concerned with personalities, and too little with underlying issues. The issues are too broad, too deep, too complex to lend themselves to dogmatic judgments as to whether this man or that man is right.

In the torrent of discussion of how we should wage war and how we should not wage it, it seems to me there is a very real danger that we are entirely losing sight of our prime national objective, which is not to wage war at all, but to achieve international peace and security.

Our aim is the same as it was when we signed the United Nations charter almost six years ago. It is the same as it was when we went to Korea. That aim is to check the aggressor, the bloody handed thief, who threatens the peace of the world. That aim is to stop the thief and stop World War III. We did not go to Korea to fight Red China. We went there to stop aggression and prevent war with Russia. We went there in common with other nations of the free world to defend a great principle, and to protect our own vital national interests in the Pacific.

But little wars breed big wars and the little war has expanded. So we find outselves in a dilemma. To end the little war that has grown bigger, shall we risk a still bigger war? Some say yes, some say no, but few there are who can understand and evaluate the infinite implications. In a democracy all of us make national policy because there can be no successful national policy without substantial unity of purpose. But, unhappily, the colors are no longer black or white for all to see. What is the effect of this or that policy, political and military, on the great prizes of Asia, India and Japan?

What is the effect of this or that policy on the vast areas of Asia hanging in the balance, committed to neither Communism nor the free world and only now tasting the heady wine of independence and nationalism which we in the West won one hundred seventy-five years ago? What is the effect in Europe, in the Middle East, in Africa? What is the effect of what we do tomorrow in Korea on the new two dimensional world of friends and foes in the United Nations, some steadfast and some quavering with fear in the long shadow of an ancient Russian imperialism behind the new facade of Communism?

To see the forest, not the trees, is difficult for us Americans whose foreign policy has been developed bit by bit, country by country, area by area: a Latin American policy, a Middle Eastern policy, a European policy, a Far Eastern policy, a Soviet policy, etc. With this genesis it is difficult for us to think of China, Iran and Yugoslavia as being part of the same problem. But now it is all one problem — a world problem — and every decision, every policy everywhere must be reached with a view to its effect, everywhere. So I say that there is a danger of over-simplification of the issues and their solution in Korea. And, if I may say so, I think we make a mistake as the great debate rumbles on, to view, as we seem to, the Soviet threat as the only threat. Many of us believed that the defeat of the Central Powers in World War I and of the Axis powers in World War II would make the world safe for democracy — or at least safe! We have got to deal with the Soviet threat, if we can, in such a way that an even more dangerous threat does not emerge thereafter, as Hitler and Tojo were a more serious threat than Kaiser Wilhelm and Emperor Franz Joseph.

The total problem we face is far larger and deeper than the power and design of the Soviet Union. The total problem involves more than a quick military decision in Korea even if one were possible. We should never again be misled into thinking that after a victory, any victory, there is peace. Because "victory" is no longer a condition, but only a word, the problems of peace are not resolved but only multiply with each successive war. So it has been and so it will be;and so we must look not alone at the whole world around us but the obscure world beyond us.

Even though we cannot foresee at this moment how and when the fighting in Korea may end, time is on our side if we use it well. We have a great productive margin over and above essential civilian requirements which can and is being allocated to defense. This margin is far greater in the United States and in the rest of the free world than it is in the Communist empire. We cannot go it alone, no nation can any longer, and our allies are gaining slowly but steadily in the will and the power to stand fast and stand together.

We need more time; at least two years to build up strength in the center and at least four years to build up strength in Western Europe. And here we face a dilemma between the need to gain time and the danger of losing positions of importance. But we would have to fight before we were prepared rather than lose positions of vital importance in Western Europe, the Far East and elsewhere.

So we must try to choose a course which minimizes the dangers of total war when we are inadequately prepared, or of losing positions we need to hold.

Thus, shorn of the clamor, the personalities and the politics, the great debate reveals our course in Korea as one of trying to minimize both of these dangers, of trying to gain time without withdrawing from a position whose loss would stimulate ambition in our enemy and defeatism among our allies. But the military mind abhors dilemma. The military instinct is to seek the clear and absolute solution to a conflict of interest. All of the training of the military is toward precision — precision in the order of battle, in logistics, in planning to attain a hypothetical end. And so it is too with the American people who are practical, who seize and solve problems one by one as they arise, and look at the world historically as so many regions with their separate problems for us.

But the conduct of foreign policy in peace cannot now approach a comparable precision. Civilian authorities are always subject to a degree of reproach and impatience from the military establishment and from people who see fragments rather than the whole. But now we must make judgments in a broad frame of reference and deal with the actual complex contingencies of foreign affairs, not hypothetical or precise situations. Indeed, the conduct of foreign policy in peace is the management of dilemmas.

It is a hard choice that we face. The risk is great no matter what course we take. But World War III is not inevitable. It can be avoided if we do not yield to appeasement of the enemy in the field or appeasement of unwise views at home, if we keep our eyes on the main objective — which is peace — if we do not lose our heads and do not permit the grave questions of national interest and destiny to degenerate into a partisan quarrel which can only divide and weaken us.

Above all we must not underestimate ourselves, either in terms of our capacity to build military and economic strength, or in terms of our spiritual and intellectual resources. We often hear it said that this or that measure will wreck the national economy. While there are, of course, limitations to overcome step by step, the task of those responsible for foreign affairs, or military affairs, is to allocate our resources in ways which will accomplish maximum results with available means.

But with a prize so great we dare not underestimate our potentialities. No one knows what the American economy is capable of. If we value our survival we should not preoccupy ourselves with limitations on building strength, but instead we should concentrate on finding ways to overcome them.

Finally, no one knows what resources of spiritual and intellectual leadership we have in this country. We have not begun to tap them. We are accustomed to meeting the needs of the free world for military and economic help. Now we are in demand as spokesmen of a better future. And we can and must meet that demand as well — patiently, confidently, in the firm faith that peace is worth the price, any price.

General MacArthur's eloquence was never more moving than when he said: "The world should have common sense enough, when it surveys the losses of two wars, to understand that war has become a method of suicide for modern civilization." And who could deny it here today in front of this Veterans Psychiatric Hospital?

RADIO REPORT TO THE PEOPLE
November 9

IT WAS MORE THAN THREE months ago that I last talked to the people of Illinois about their state government. That periodical report was shortly after the adjournment of the legislature and I spoke about the results of the session, emphasizing, among other things, the great importance of the bills making possible, at last, the rebuilding of our highways. Through the courtesy of this station I want to speak to you now about that, and also about some noteworthy new developments in other areas.

For example, two distinct forward strides have been taken of late in our welfare services. Illinois has opened at the Peoria State Hospital the first center in the middle west for the care and treatment of mentally ill children. This unique hospital unit will treat psychoses among children six to fourteen years old — who heretofore have been mingled with adult patients at the various large state mental hospitals. We feel confident that this new and very attractive care and treatment center for children will result in the earlier correction of emotional disturbances, and that many boys and girls will be rescued from a dreary lifetime in mental institutions and returned to normal active lives.

At Galesburg, where two years ago we acquired a large Federal wartime hospital at nominal cost, we are establishing an institution for the care of elderly mental patients and for research in the diseases of the older people. The task of remodelling the buildings and assembling a competent staff of psychiatrists, technicians and nurses, is approaching completion. There we hope to gain new knowledge about the care and treatment of persons whose commitment is attributable largely to senility. Illinois is pioneering in this field of research, which is becoming more and more important as increasing numbers of aged people are being sent to mental institutions largely because there is nowhere else to send them. Here again our objective is to get them out of the institutions and return as many as possible to their homes and families or to more normal environments.

The importance of these efforts can be readily understood when we realize that half of the hospital beds in the nation are now occupied by the mentally ill, and the thirty- seven million dollars per year it costs us taxpayers just to operate our hospitals represents one of our major financial burdens.

In the area of state finances I am happy to report that our house is in good order. Revenues have been running almost exactly at the levels estimated when the budget was drafted almost a year ago, although the picture is complicated by perplexing uncertainties of the economic situation. We are applying still tighter safeguards in the financial management of the various state agencies. We are operating in the black.

But in order to maintain a balanced budget it was necessary for me to veto forty-two million dollars of appropriations which the legislature voted in excess of the budget I submitted. Those ranged from the questionable "Christmas tree" bills, through which state funds were formerly appropriated for certain private organizations, to numerous and generous appropriations for bridges, roads, commissions and various other projects.

Some of these appropriations were for desirable purposes; others were of the political "log-rolling" type. In either case the failure to veto them would have been inimical to sound fiscal policy and would have committed the state to expenditures in excess of our estimated revenue. In these days of rising costs and higher federal taxes for the essential needs of national defense we can't even afford some desirable things, let alone luxuries.

In the case of the special appropriations for bridges and local roads, amounting to over twenty million dollars, it does not seem to me sound public policy for the legislature to determine when and where roads and bridges shall be built by the process of exchanging courtesy votes. It may be good politics at home, but on that basis our road system would not reflect traffic needs so much as political influence. We have had too much of that already, and I think highway improvements should be made in accordance with priorities established by the Division of Highways on the basis of traffic requirements, present and future. If many localities are disappointed I am sorry and I'll have to suffer the consequences, but I think most people will agree that the only proper way to spend everybody's money is *for* everybody. In no other way can we avoid the errors and abuses of the past.

The financial soundness of any enterprise, whether it is business or government, depends not only on the relationship between income and expense but also on the integrity and sound judgment reflected in its financial operations.

I have, therefore, placed continuing emphasis upon the effectiveness of the Department of Finance as a medium for the planning and the control of state expenditures, and also for improving the standards of management in the state service. A case in point is the Division of Purchases, which buys everything from apples to automobiles and spends many millions of your taxes. State purchasing should and must be a purely business operation. The state must buy the best merchandise it can afford for the lowest price, and it must get what it pays for.

It was this consideration which prompted the creation the other day of a distinguished committee of purchasing directors from private business and public agencies to advise the Department of Finance on procedures, standards and personnel training arrangements aimed at insuring that prices and quality of merchandise — not "influence" — shall govern state buying.

The growing public concern about morality in public life is a healthy trend, and if it is sustained — as I hope it is —it will lead to generally higher standards of public service and better law enforcement. There is a close relationship, for example, between our efforts to strengthen the management of our financial affairs and our parallel effort to bring about better law enforcement. Both rest upon the integrity and concept of duty of officials, employees and also the citizens with whom they deal, because you must remember that public servants don't corrupt each other; it is the citizens who corrupt them. A mutual sense of responsibility is the indispensable element in the best possible government in a far from perfect world.

We are making steady progress toward improved law enforcement in Illinois. In Cook County there is now much wholesome activity. Downstate, which includes one hundred counties, we have had admirable results in some counties, mediocre performance in others, and poor enforcement in some. But I believe that more and more the inexorable pressure of public opinion is being brought to bear on local law enforcement officials to do the job for which they were elected.

Let me cite an example. Since the state police began their raids on commercial gambling at my direction in May 1950 there has been a tremendous drop in slot machines in the seventy-six counties of the southern internal revenue district of Illinois. In 1948 there were about 8,400 of these machines registered for federal taxation in those counties. In the first three months of the present tax year, beginning July 1, the number fell to 1783. In other words, there are about one-fifth as many accounted for now as there were before the raids began.

But there is a disturbing element in the picture. Evidently only about seven per cent of the machines still operating, of which the Federal government has a record, are in taverns or other public places. Most of them are in private clubs and organizations.

This would seem to indicate that many of our most reputable and influential citizens, often critical of public morals and the breakdown in local law enforcement, see nothing inconsistent in violating the law themselves, or at least countenancing such violations in their private clubs. By such self indulgence many useful citizens sterilize their power and influence to demand and get faithful service from local officials. A double standard of law enforcement and law observance is dangerous in a country dedicated to the principle of equal treatment for all and special privileges for none.

But, in short, we are making progress toward better law enforcement, and I believe we will make more as people come to understand that the responsibility for fostering respect for our laws rests upon them as well as the officials, and that failure at home inevitably leads to the surrender of local self government to higher levels of authority — the very centralization of power which we all deplore and oppose.

But, happily, law enforcement is still primarily a local responsiblity in Illinois, whereas the responsiblity for providing a good highway system is one that rests primarily with the state.

What we are doing today to save our road system, to restore it to its once leading place among the states, represents the biggest public improvement project Illinois has undertaken since the original hard road program of the Twenties.

Everyone who has had occasion to drive about the state in recent weeks is aware of the accelerated activity in road construction and repair. The trucks and graders and bulldozers are at work in many places.

But the road program can't reach its peak until 1954 because we are carrying it out on a pay-as-you-go basis—without borrowing and paying interest charges — and the Highway revenue bills passed by the legislature will not yield their maximum returns until 1954. The gasoline tax, of which the state gets about a third, was raised from three to four cents August 1 this year, and will not go to five cents until January 1, 1953. Truck license fees were increased twenty million dollars a year, effective in 1952 and will go to twenty-eight million dollars a year in 1954. But these increased truck fees are currently threatened by lawsuits in what appears to be a major effort to invalidate them. We hope for an early and favorable decision. Otherwise the restoration of our state highways will be seriously hampered.

As I say, we are stepping up the tempo of road work as the new money becomes available. Up to a week ago, 232 separate highway contracts in

1951 have exceeded in number and dollar volume the largest previous total in our history. During the last two months of this year, and in 1952, the Highway Division will award some 400 additional projects all over Illinois.

Under the old level of highway revenues — based on the 3-cent gas tax and our very low truck license fees — we had about thirty million dollars a year to spend on the highways, including federal aid. During the next two years highway contracts will approximate an average of seventy-seven millions a year, or two and a half times the old rate.

This refers only to the state highways. It does not include the shares of the gas tax that go to the cities, counties and, starting in 1952, for the first time, to the townships, to assist them in the construction and maintenance of our now inadequate local road system.

When you realize the magnitude of the task we face, the large sum we should have available in the next two years doesn't seem so large. A careful survey of every mile of our primary state highway system has shown that seventy per cent of our present mileage will be worn out or deficient by 1960. Fortunately, most of this total of more than 7,000 miles can be corrected by resurfacing, or widening and resurfacing, the existing pavements. The remainder involves new construction and additional traffic lanes.

And let me say here that it is going to be our policy to save existing pavements wherever we can, rather than to build expensive new ones. All road work is terribly expensive these days, due to the increased value of the property we have to acquire and the steep rises in the cost of labor and materials of all kinds. Resurfacing an old road usually costs one-third to one-half as much as new construction, and there is such a vast amount of work to do it is imperative that we stretch our highway dollars as far as we can.

By December the Division of Highways will publish the detailed plans for the 1952 highway program. This is an innovation in state highway administration; it is a part of our policy for making known fully to the people, in advance, just what projects are to be undertaken and where.

We face the future confident that we have the best planned, the best balanced, the most equitably financed highway program Illinois ever had. Getting the job done, and done well, is of the utmost importance to the economic and social welfare of all our people — now and in the future. It is the dawn of a new day for the Illinois motorist. It's up to us to do the job as well, as rapidly, as honestly and as economically as we possibly can.

I'm afraid this has been a dull talk, but I am grateful to you who have listened to it. It is your government here in Springfield, and the more you know about what we are doing and why, the better it will be for you who supply the money, and for us whom you have entrusted to spend it honestly and wisely.

DEDICATION OF SOUTHERN ILLINOIS UNIVERSITY TRAINING SCHOOL, CARBONDALE
November 17

DOUBTS BRED OF MISUNDERSTANDING complicate most all public issues. But with better communication comes better understanding, and therefore, better thinking. Thus, the ability to communicate our thoughts by the written or spoken word, to teach young people to think, to evaluate, and judge for themselves the values in life has become a vast need.

The other day I ran across a little prayer which expresses my thought:

"God give me the patience to accept that which cannot be changed. Give me the courage to change that which can and should be changed. And above all, give me the wisdom to know which is which."

When all is said and done, the successful educational program is one that teaches young people to think clearly, to express themselves lucidly, and to judge discerningly. This implies, of course, complete freedom of thought and expression. But we cannot ignore the ugly fact that freedom of thought and expression are sometimes unpopular, especially in times of national peril. For peril breeds tension, and tension, repression. In these days of anxiety and doubt, as Lincoln said: "Every foul bird comes out and every dirty reptile rises up." careless inquistion, irresponsible accusation, raise the spectre of organized thought to mock the spirit of liberty.

It is little wonder then that people become fearful and timid. Social scientists have to be careful in their research and in announcing their findings; qualified citizens hesitate to risk their reputations in government service, where it is always open season. Dr. Robert M. Hutchins, former Chancellor of the University of Chicago, has felt impelled to henceforth join no organization, even one whose sole objective is the preservation and perpetuation of Mother's Day!

The tragedy, of course, is that epithet, confusion and suspicion which have become so commonplace in our public life are cloaked in patriotism and cultivated in the guise of the defense of freedom. Washington had a pertinent phrase: "The impostures of pretended patriotism." The only defense is the truth, but people must be able to penetrate the sham and hypocrisy and see the truth.

I suppose we always will have demagogues in public life. They may even serve some useful purpose — if only to demonstrate that democracy has its booby traps too. These are not too great a hazard if only our free system of public education — the greatest cultural device of our civilization — is always free; if the student is always free to acquire knowledge, to accept ideas or to reject them, straight, uncolored and uncorrupted.

It is becoming increasingly clear to us that extraordinary demands will be made on the human resources of the United States in the years ahead. There are shortages in trained personnel. There are shortages in the educational facilities to turn out the trained personnel. But we have the raw materials in the native talent of our youth. We need only to discover and constantly develop that talent. We cannot match our potential enemies in numbers, but we can surpass them in brains. We have the kind of social and political system that enables us to surpass them in every sphere except numbers, through the free and full cultivation of the intellectual capacities of our people.

The important thing to remember is that we shall continue to prosper only as we develop and relate our human resources to the growing needs of society. It is no part of democratic doctrine to waste talent or to tolerate the pseudo-luxury of its non-development. You are proving this here at Southern, in this new temple of teaching. We are proving here that truth is the most powerful weapon against tyranny and despotism. Time will reveal that the intellectual paralysis of the people, which is the indispensable ingredient of totalitarianism, is more deadly to the Soviet system than military weapons.

So we can take heart and face the future unafraid! Our basic ways are right; we need only cultivate them. Our virtues outweigh our shortcomings. We need only to keep on growing, to hold fast to truth wherever it may lead, to keep the pioneering spirit, extending it mightily and rapidly in the realm of the humanities, the arts and the sciences.

For, if it is true that the human race has all but exhausted its margin for error, then we must look to education to provide quickly men and women qualified to make the decisions on which the survival of democratic values rest. In this century, when history moves on the double quick, the long range problems of education have become a short range necessity.

Sometimes I'm glad I'm just a politician and not an educator!

1952

I 'M DEEPLY GRATEFUL TO you Senator Lewis for your moving introduction. I thought for a moment that you were going to introduce Benjamin Franklin at the conclusion.

I'm frank to say I hardly know why I'm here this evening. The last time I came to the Robinson Country Club, the departing gesture was the presentation to me of a blank sheet of paper by three charming young girls who asked if I would give them my autograph. I promptly complied, covered with confusion, and I hope modest blushes, and then they turned the paper over and I found that I had signed a statment which read as follows: "All slot machines in this Club are reserved for my personal use."

Well the fact of the matter is, I've always been sceptical of speaking at Chamber of Commerce banquets. But we Democrats can seldom resist the opportunity to speak before a group like this. I think it's due to the fact that we probably all suffer from an inferiority complex and that we're glad to associate with respectable businessmen now and then.

Senator Lewis has suggested that perhaps I could speak extemporaneously. But I've always been suspicious of extemporaneous speeches. There was an occasion when I first got into politics that a governor of another state—an elderly gentleman—said to me: "Now young man, I should be very careful about casual remarks. It was only a few months ago that I made a casual remark. I announced to the press that I had strained my back lifting a window in the executive mansion. When it appeared in the opposition newspaper, it said that Governor X had been obliged to cancel all of his appointments for a week because he strained his back lifting a *widow* in the executive mansion."

As businessmen, you have to worry about your budgets, and so do I. I remember the young bridegroom who was worried about his budget because every time he contrived to make both ends meet, his wife moved the ends. Well that's somewhat the trouble a public servant faces. My problem however, is preparing a budget for two years and then getting it approved by a legislature that sometimes isn't too friendly. But I'm glad to say that I've had the most satisfactory relationship between a Democratic Governor and a Republican legislature during this last session. We've probably produced more, and more important legislation than in any previous session of our General Assembly in modern times.

The Democrats indeed complained at the end of the session that the Republicans had stolen my program. It reminded me of the story of the young American couple who took a honeymoon in France and were driving through the chateau country when their car broke down. The boy got out and went under the car to fix it. And soon the girl got impatient and crawled under to join him. A long time evidently went past when he felt a tug at his shoulder and when he looked up there was a French gendarme who said, "Pardon, monsieur. It is not just that there are four hundred peasants on the hills watching. Nor is it that there are twelve cars waiting to pass. It is, monsieur, that your car has been stolen."

Well, I enjoyed the romance with the Republican legislature and I'm very glad they stole my program and that it was virtually all enacted.

You men and women are identified with the business world. You are typical of the still greater number of businesspeople throughout Illinois and the nation who have banded together in associations like this one to further not just your own interests but those of the community. In considerable part, your job consists of improving the relationship between the business community and the public at large. My job is somewhat the same. Part of it is to inform people about what their state government is doing, to demonstrate that it is seeking earnestly and honestly to promote their welfare.

Your interests coincide with the public interests and so do mine. We're all on the same team, even if we don't belong to the same party. What is good for business is good for government and vice versa. Neither could do without the other even in normal times. In today's world, when free government is fighting for its very life, there is a greater than ever need for closer cooperation between people and the leaders of thought and action and their government.

Government and its employees ought not to be exempt from criticism, far from it. It is from free and open discussion, from close and continuous scrutiny, from differences of opinion, that public directed decisions will ultimately flow. And public opinion in the last analysis is the sovereign of us all.

But criticism should not in itself be an end. It should be specific rather than general; it should be constuctive rather than generally destructive. One of the most disturbing factors in our own contemporary public life it seems to me is the widespread practice of indictment by generalization, and conviction by accusation.

For example, all government employees should not be condemned for the spectacular sins of a few. Yet that is unhappily sometimes the prevailing tendency. Unless we resist this growing practice as unhealthy and unjust, we will undermine the very faith in free institutions we are striving to uphold the world over, and we will further depreciate the coinage of government just when we need better men in government so desperately. We ought to keep reminding ouselves that in our democracy, government depends on the consent of the governed. If the confidence of the people in the competent, conscientious and honest people who staff our government is destroyed, that consent could be imperceptibly withdrawn with implications which we cannot forsee with any complacency.

Many well meaning individuals and organizations in addition resort to hammering at government officials as a group in hopes of achieving some immediate result. Their aim is not to bring permanent injury to our governmental system, but merely to gain some immediate end, whether it be an election or the enactment of some legislation. But the cumulative effect can be damaging and enduring.

The other day I ran across this:

There is thoughout the United States a widespread and vigorous propaganda against government and government service. This is not the attitude of anarchists or radicals, but of conservatives.

There are those high in our industrial life who openly take the position that the best government is the worst. And there are others not so high who constantly scoff and sneer at all government enterprise. I don't hesitate to say that the most expensive luxury in America today is the widespread opinion that government is necessarily weak, ignorant, corrupt, and contemptible. This attitude not only costs us billions, but billions of dollars annually because it poisons the springs of government interest, enthusiasm, and service. This boycott of government and public life makes difficult the recruitment of the personnel necessary for government. It invites spoilsmen and racketeers, and drives away many of those who might best serve the state. It produces high costs and lower achievement levels.

Government is not a theft, or a blight, or a necessary evil. It has an important and real function to perform in modern life. Men are not payed merely in dollars and cents, but in terms of social regard and of respect. They will work as hard to be well thought of as to be well paid.

The continued condemnation of the government and its agents will tend to discredit the public service at the very moment when it might well be built up and made still more seviceable to the community.

Students of government know from long experience and observation that there is no road to effective government that does not recognize the need for building up respect for honest and efficient public service. Undiscriminating attacks on all government and all public servants alike constitutes the certain way to costly and inefficient public service.

Now if any of you should imagine that the author of those words was a prominent and worried Democratic politician, let me disabuse you hastily. The author was Charles E. Merrill, Dean of Political Scientists in the United States, and now professor emeritus.

Public servants who violate the public trust should be punished severly and promptly. One dishonest public official is one too many. And so is one dishonest private citizen as well. As a matter of fact, when you see it for a while from the government side of the fence, where I have been sitting but three short years, when you see how many private citizens there are who violate the law, who corrupt officials, who use pressure, or preferment, and do it with shameless persistence, I sometimes wonder if the ethical standards of public life are not actually higher than in private life and in private business.

After all, public business is conducted in a goldfish bowl. Most acts of public officials can be closely scrutinized if we are vigilant. And that's the way it should be. But this circumstance poses difficulties. To staff government positions with the highest type of worker, it is first necessary to beat down this barrage of loose talk, of mistrust and derision which discourages many people from entering public life. Any public administrator will tell you how difficult it is to persuade really talented and outstanding young people to enter public service with the thought of making it a career when the inducement elsewhere is often greater, and the reward is too often criticism, ingratitude, and abuse.

Here is a job in which the businessman can do his part. Government needs business thinking and business leadership. Business must recognize that out-producing and out-budgeting all the other nations does not in itself ensure peace and security or even prosperity.

Government needs brains too. It needs them more than business and particularly in a time of violence, revolution, and turmoil like the generation in which we are destined to live.

This is the "big game" that we are playing, and the outcome is vital to us. No team can be successful unless there is mutual trust among its members. None of you could operate your business without confidence in your employees, and neither can the government. Instead of creating imaginary schisms between business and government, I wish we could work for more understanding and greater teamwork, certainly at the state level, where there is literally almost nothing whatever to divide us on party lines, and where there is every reason for the closest cooperation and the utmost understanding.

Whether state government is good or bad, efficient, or disorderly and wasteful, honest or corrupt, is your concern. Because you pay the bills. And those who have the most have the biggest stake.

I've been in elected public office just three years. I've had to learn much, and learn it the hard way. Not as an observer, but under the guns with the sole responsibility for the decisions. It's not been easy. Indeed, much of it I have found hard, uninteresting, and unpleasant. But there have been many compensations too —the satisfaction of a little progress here and there. The satisfaction of attracting some good people to state government and of having had an active part in the affairs of my generation. These are great rewards. And I have learned something too in this process; something of the virtues of patience, and hope, and of persistence. I know what the apostle meant who said "We glory in tribulations, knowing that tribulation waketh patience, patience experience, and experience hope."

My hope is for a lively, active, informed participation in the affairs of Illinois by more people like yourselves. And my greatest reward and pleasure in this difficult task is the opportunity to meet with so many people who will listen to me talk, even about the dullest aspects of state government.

As someone once said to me, "You always get around to that stuff. You're sort of like the Australian bushman who bought a new boomerang and then spent the rest of his life trying to get rid of the old one."

BANQUET FOR THE FOURTH DEGREE
KNIGHTS OF COLUMBUS, CHICAGO
February 25

THROUGHOUT OUR national existence, indeed from the earliest settlement, America has been a symbol of hope wherever men have aspired to be free and stand erect. But today the great American experiment is face to face with those who manipulate and toy with symbols of democracy, who would undermine our prestige, who in the the hot war of ideas offer up as a program the paradox of democracy through dictatorship, liberty through oppression, justice through tyranny, and freedom through thralldom.

I believe that the effectiveness of the Soviet Union has been chiefly due to one thing: it has made the miserable everywhere conscious of their misery. It has given distorted impetus to the newborn urgings and aspirations of suppressed and subjugated peoples. It has stuck a mischievous finger into almost every country, including our own.

But it isn't necessary for me to remind you that our supreme task is to recognize it for what it is and meet it with all the intelligence and resources at our command. For whatever else it is, communism is a conviction and flaming faith to many mortals. And our job is to match and beat it with even deeper faith, conviction and passion for our principles.

The desperate war years and the challenge of Korea have brought us closer than ever to the other nations of the world which cherish their independence and man's freedom. Here in America, in spite of the partisan discords which are an integral part of our political system, I think we have come to a better understanding of the common enemy and the perils that confront us. We are learning, I think, that the answer to communism is democracy; not less democracy, or just enough, but more. And democracy means preserving for every individual, regardless of his color, his religion, or his nationality the same rights, privileges and opportunities that others enjoy. It means setting an example of the very things for which your own organization stands — charity, unity, fraternity and patriotism.

But lest you think I came here tonight to talk only of the difficult problems that confront us in world affairs, let me reassure you otherwise. My intention was to make some brief observations on another subject, close to home, that concerns me very much because I'm in it. It also concerns you because you are in it too. That subject is government, and specifically the level of morality that exists in our public life today.

It isn't exactly a new subject these days. In fact it is all too familiar. The papers and the air waves are full of it and everyone is talking about it.

People are saying we have had too many examples of unfaithfulness and dishonesty among public officials. Some even say we are witnessing a breakdown in the whole moral structure of our country which could lead, as it has before, to disaster, and ultimately the oblivion of the greatest constitutional democracy ever devised by man.

Certainly we have had too many evidences of dishonesty and faithlessness to public trust. One dishonest public official is one too many. Corruption is treason. And I would go further and say that this experience is doubly unfortunate because high standards of public service were never more important than now. The challenge to America is world wide. The free world looks to us for leadership. The greatest weapon we have in the struggle is public and private morality. Anything that dulls the edge of that weapon weakens our cause and our position in the eyes of the world. Everything depends on America. Yet at the peak of her power, shouldering such monstrous responsibilities as few nations have ever borne, the personal and public moral life of our people discloses a shame to which none of us can be blind.

But, at the same time, there is much evidence that we are not on a toboggan slide to perdition.Indeed we may be experiencing a healthy revival of public consciousness that will strengthen our democratic structure. We may be actually in the process of taking a forward, not a backward, step in the direction of higher ethical standards in public as well as private life.

Whether things are better or worse than at other times, I frankly don't know. There are many here tonight much better able to judge of that than I. But I do know that we have more publicity about wrong doing, and a greater public awareness of it, because our media of communications are better. And human weakness is nothing new. Shakespeare took note of it in the familiar lines: "The evil men do lives after them; the good is oft interred with their bones."

It seems as though the most creative, enterprising periods in human history have always been troubled and disorderly. The sixteenth century witnessed the flowering of the Renaissance, but a great contemporary, Erasmus, called that stirring era "the excrement of the ages." So too the eighteenth century which we regard as one of the most creative, with the American and French Revolutions, was to Rousseau "this great rottenness in which we live."

I take some comfort from the historical and contemporary view of violent and disturbed eras. But comfort, courage and hope are not complacency. And I say root out the wrongdoers, wherever they may be, and punish them. And public censure ought not to be confined just to willful violations of our laws. It should extend to those who violate the moral code, for legality is not a synonym for morality.

But government can't do this job alone. This is everybody's responsibility. As Dr. Harry Emerson Fosdick said here in Chicago just the other day: "Government can do nothing for us, except as we citizens put into government the character which we ourselves first of all possess. All government is like a pump; and the water it pumps is the intellectual, moral and spiritual life of the people — no better, no worse."

This thought that elevating moral standards in our private and public life is the responsibility of each individual was eloquently expressed in November of last year by the Bishops of the United States in their admirable joint statement issued on the occasion of the National Catholic Welfare Conference.

Many of you are familiar with that statement. It drew a parallel between our situation today and the Roman empire fifteen centuries ago, threatened outwardly by barbarism and inwardly by moral decline. To meet these twin perils the Bishops called for a universal reawakening of responsibility on the part of every citizen, a recognition that there can be no double standard of morality, and that in all human affairs only "what conforms with God's will is right." I want to quote that part of the statement dealing with morality and politics:

> In politics, the principle that 'anything goes' simply because people are thought not to expect any high degree of honor in politicians is grossly wrong. We have to recover that sense of personal obligation on the part of the voter and that sense of public trust on the part of the elected official which give meaning and dignity to political life. Those who are selected for office by their fellow men are entrusted with grave responsibilities. They have been selected not for self-enrichment but for conscientious public service. In their speech and in their actions they are bound by the same laws of justice and charity which bind private individuals in every other sphere of human activity. Dishonesty, slander, detraction and defamation of character are as truly transgressions of God's commandments when resorted to by men in political life as they are for all other men.

Those words seem so obvious they hardly need repetition. But they must be repeated over and over again. Too few people are willing to work for government with the same disinterest and devotion they give to charity, for example.

Every public executive knows that finding competent, trustworthy people for responsible positions in government is a difficult task. And he knows that in spite of all precautions his confidence will occasionally be misplaced; a few will prove unfaithful to their trust. That is the risk he must run. It is the realization he must live with constantly. And there is another old reality — too many people are ready and anxious to corrupt public officials for private gain. The people are the water in the well.

Just the other day a school teacher in Kalamazoo, Michigan, wrote me a letter in which she drew an interesting analogy. In part this is what she wrote:

"You have obstacles, frustrations, disappointments.Perhaps governing a city, state, or nation is something like keeping house. Sometimes the plumbing wears out, the furnace blows up or the servants are caught stealing. But a good master can make repairs, discharge dishonest servants, or do whatever is necessary to clean house and make it operate efficiently."

She was illustrating the point I would like to make here — that today's agitation about moral standards, about evidences of untrustworthiness among some in our public house, does not mean that the house is tumbling down any more than does faulty plumbing or a worn out furnace.

How then do we combat moral breakdown and political corruption? Let us learn where we stand, objectively and thoroughly, neither hiding nor exaggerating ugly facts. Having learned the facts, let us expose and punish the guilty. And in doing so let us keep in mind that with all our imperfections we are making epic strides toward building here in America a society where as never before men and women can live at their best. Let us use our findings of moral laxity to clear the ground for still greater growth; good will conquer evil.

The point I would emphasize is that the phase through which we are passing now will, I believe, be looked upon in the long view of history as an eddy in the strong stream of progress toward higher moral health to which we aspire. Indeed I believe it is this constantly rising standard that is largely responsible for the increasing emphasis that is being placed upon corruption, whether it be in our public or our private life.

As long as it does not condemn the innocent unjustly, this trend is healthy. Our whole social system demands confidence in each other. I once heard a foreign visitor say he had just observed in America one of the most wonderful things he had ever seen. He had seen the bottles of milk and the newspapers on the back porches of apartment buildings, with never a thought that anyone would steal them. That's but one small example of the reliance which we have, and must have, on each other's integrity. Likewise, government must be based upon the people's reliance in its integrity. If that is destroyed, the damage is difficult to repair.

That is why I have said before, and I say again, that overemphasis upon moral corruption — to the point where its dimensions are magnified beyond their true proportions — can be dangerous. That would be the case, if, as Justice Charles Evans Hughes said at the time of the Teapot Dome scandals, it were to seriously impair public confidence in the fundamental democratic processes. I've heard people say, and no doubt you have too, that they don't want to have anything to do with politics. And that's a sad situation, because public service should attract not the mediocre but the best in a government by the consent of the governed.

And now I would like to say a word about what has occurred right here in Chicago in the last couple of weeks. We have witnessed an unusual example of public indignation growing out of a brutal murder. Whatever were the circumstances of the crime, it has served to bring violently and emphatically to public attention an undesirable influence which has no place in the public life of Chicago and of Illinois.

That influence isn't new. We have seen the cynical symptoms for a long time. It has been spreading, and like aggression, it must be arrested before it is too late. The job calls for some major surgery. It calls for positive action, not just on one front, but on many.

The political parties have a responsibility in the public interest which they purport to represent, and in their self interest as well. Because, as someone put it, "First you get power, then you use it, then you abuse it, then you lose it." The police, the prosecutors, the parties and the public officials all have work to do. But the job won't be done or stay done without a sustained public opinion, not just a passing flurry of indignation, but a continuing crusade — that will drive this element out of public places, whether it be in the city hall, the county building, or the statehouse. I hope Chicago's civic conscience and self-respect will stay aroused this time.

Perhaps the mechanics of the system by which we elect some officers, ward committeemen and members of the legislature, for example, need overhauling. Personally, I have never looked with favor on the present system in legislative elections which permits the senatorial committee of each party, in each district, to limit the number of candidates of that party to be nominated in the primary. Too often it discourages candidates from running for the legislature. It restricts the choice of the voters. In some districts they have no real choice at all. Of the 153 members of the Illinois House of Representatives to be elected this year, eighty-four will be assured of election without a contest in November because they will be the only nominees. That situation applies in twenty-eight of the fifty-one legislative districts in the state, including the so-called "West side bloc" districts in Chicago. I would prefer a system which would give the voters a freer, wider choice without destroying all guarantees of adequate minority representation.

And also I have pointed out on many occasions that the legislature has been remiss for years in ignoring the mandate of the State Constitution that it remap the legislative districts every ten years to equalize their population.

That is one step that can and should be taken not only to break up rotten boroughs but also to give our citizens something like equal individual representation in the legislature. This isn't a matter of purely local concern to Chicago. The people of downstate Illinois have a stake in the fight too. Sectional jealousies should not overburden the vital interests of all the people of Illinois. Moreover, the downstate need have no fear that it would surrender complete control of the legislature to the metropolitan area. We could arrive at a plan for legislative redistricting under which control of the two houses of the General Assembly would be divided between Cook County and downstate.

No man or woman should ever feel that he is personally helpless. All the evidence of history demonstrates otherwise. A handful of prophets changed the moral course of the world. A comparatively few leaders elevated the religious philosophies of millions of men. The founding fathers, to which we refer so often, were few, yet they liberated and charted the glorious destiny of this country for centuries.

Every one of us has a vote, and with it a responsibility. The citadel of democracy will not be held by the vigorous assertion of right alone, but by the discharge of duties as well. If, for lack of courage, or interest, or genuine patriotism, we do not utilize our political power then we betray the privilege of self government. And we also open wide the doors of political corruption.

And, finally, the decent people of Chicago out-number the indecent by the same top-heavy proportion as the honorable men and women in public service out-number the corrupt. The people can win all their battles if they will.

CITIZENS SCHOOLS COMMITTEE, CHICAGO
March 3

I COME BEFORE YOU NOW, as I did four years ago, to think with you on a problem of overwhelming importance—the provision of proper educational opportunities for the children of our state. In 1952, even more than in 1948, the attention of our citizens is largely preoccupied with the distractions of the national and international scene. We sense the gravity of the issues that are at stake in the threats to our way of life that appear from hostile forces both without and within our country.

This struggle is much more than the clash of arms on distant battlefields; it is primarily a struggle for the minds of men, in this and in the next generation at least.We are here today because we realize — you and I—that it is in the schoolrooms of the world that the truly meaningful questions confronting humanity will be finally answered.

The conduct of public education is, in a very unique fashion, a major concern of the chief executive of this state. On the one hand, public education is a vital function of our public life in which the Federal government has not, to any large degree, intruded. There is some federal assistance to vocational education, to school lunches, and in some other minor and temporary areas of the work of our common schools. But on the whole, the kind of public schools we have in Illinois has been determined by our own people. In a very real sense, as has been pointed out by most educational experts, we do not have a public school system in America, we have what the Council of State Government called "The Forty-eight School Systems of America." Thus the Governor of Illinois becomes, whether he wishes to or not, a part-time superintendent of schools for his state's system and finds, whether he wishes it or not, that a part of his time and energy, and a very substantial part of his state's budget, is devoted to public education. And I hasten to add, that this Governor at least, has no illusions and makes no pretense of being an educational expert. It was said of a British Prime Minister that whenever he was asked a policy question he couldn't answer he replied: "We will appoint a Royal Commission to make a thorough investigation of the matter." I have not yet held office for a single term but have already appointed three commissions to study school problems. Two were temporary, designed to deal with specific and immediate problems confronting the legislature and the schools at the 1949 session of the General Assembly which convened simultaneously with my taking office. The third was something quite different. It is the Illinois School Problems Commission established by the

the legislature at my recommendation to carry on a continuing study of school needs—to function as a permanent advisory board to the legislature.

I think the creation of this new agency was one of the most constructive single steps that has been taken in education in this state. As to the Commission, my pride of paternity is shameless. Let me tell you why. When I took office Illinois had no agency responsible for the expert consideration, formulation and recommendation of a comprehensive legislative program for the schools. Nor had any provision been made for continuity in the expert consideration of our many and complex school problems. That void has now been filled. The School Problems Commission is non-partisan. It includes experienced school people as well as legislators. It has provided a forum through which the interested groups can air their problems and suggestions and get them carefully considered. Incidentally, public hearings have been started by this Commission in preparation for the 1953 legislative session. Now, for the first time, the Commission carefully prepares in advance of the legislature's convening, not only much legislation, but an objective estimate of the amount of state funds needed by the schools for the next biennium. That is a significant point. Heretofore this vitally important question of how much the schools should get from the state treasury was left to political trading, to pressure and counter-pressure, to partisan maneuvering and recrimination in the heat of legislative sessions. That never was a rational way to deal with so serious an issue, and in the light of constantly growing educational needs it would be both inadequate and dangerous now and in the future. Many of you are familiar with the report of the Commission and its approach to the determination of what consititutes a good foundation program and the steps by which the state can contribute to it consistent with its other responsibilities.

That the Commission has been fortunate in its direction is demonstrated by the splendid cooperation it received from the legislature in 1951. The first Chairman was Representatives Walter O. Edwards, of Danville, who happens to be a Democrat, and the present Chairman is Representative Charles Claybaugh, of Champaign, a Republican. Both are longtime students of educational problems in this state. And the Commission was wise in enlisting the technical counsel of one of the ablest school men in Illinois, Dr. Richard Browne, who is on leave of absence from Illinois State Normal University and who at the present time is serving as executive officer of the Teachers College Board. He was Research Director of the School Problems Commission and in my judgment is entitled to the respect and thanks of everyone interested in this fundamental problem.

In short, there has been established machinery through which we can resolve our school problems now and in the future in an orderly, objective, intelligent way as distinguished from the former haphazard approach in which political expediency, lobbying and attrition were too often the rule. I hope the school system can be kept in this wholesome status for keeps.

Illinois has placed an unusually large share of the responsibility for the management, control, and financial support of the schools in the local school districts, in the places where the vigor and strength of democracy is nurtured and strengthened. But the Illinois Constitution declares it to be the responsibility of the state to assure a good education for all of the children. This result can be achieved only when the state assumes active and constructive leadership in the key areas of school organization and finance. The state must make it possible for each school district to be properly organized, adequately financed, and intelligently administered. The rest is the responsibity of the educators, the parents, and other local citizens.

Four years ago, as a candidate for Governor, I solemnly committed my administration to a conscientious, earnest attempt to provide such leadership for our schools as it is proper for the state to assume. It is gratifying, in 1952, to be given so many assurances of the redemption of that pledge.

Now what does this increased state contribution to the schools mean to the average citizen? It means, in many districts, that property taxes for school purposes have not had to be increased to meet higher educational costs. In other districts, tax rates have gone up, but not as much as they would have had to had not the state aid level been raised. That is the case here in Chicago. It means better educational opportunities, better school facilities. It has enabled the legislature, as it did in 1951, to raise substantially the minimum salaries for teachers.

More significant than the amount of State Aid provided even, is the recent sharp increase in the equalization level. This level, in the formula used to distribute state funds, establishes the type of educational opportunity which the state underwrites. When I took office this level was set at $90 per year for each child in the elementary schools and $100 per year for each child in high school. Today the level stands at $160 for both elementary and high school children. This sharp increase was possible partly because of increased state aid but also because we were willing to ask the local citizens to make a heavier contribution. This was accomplished through a substantial increase in the rate which the local districts must levy to qualify for state aid.

These, and many other parts, combined into a symmetrical school program of which Illinois can feel proud. But it would be unbecoming, albeit characteristic, of candidates for public office, if I failed to note that it developed from the intelligently cooperative work of many agencies over a period of years considerably longer than my term in public office.

There is much work yet to be done. And I know I can count on your help to get it done. Some of our schools are not yet properly organized. Illinois has not yet faced the school needs that will develop during the next two decades as school attendance reaches all time record levels. These children have already been born. They are beginning to enter the primary grades. As they move along through the school system during the coming years the school population is certain to rise. Will there be adequate school buildings to house these additional pupils? Will there be qualified teachers for them? Will we have overcrowded classrooms, half-day shifts, inefficient and deteriorated buildings, teachers with substandard qualifications? Or will our school system go forward toward better education for all its children?

Those questions cannot be answered by any single official, department or commission. We will answer them, and answer them in the proper way, only by the persistent, diligent, intelligent cooperation of the various agencies, official and unofficial, which deal with education.

Nor should we lose sight of the quality of the education and its product. We have learned much about how children learn. We have been dedicated for more than a century to the proposition that education is, in the words of the Northwest Ordinance of 1787 "necessary to the good government and happiness of mankind." It is now our obligation to implement our basic convictions on the fundamental goals of education in a free society. The Illinois School Problems Commission reported a year ago:

> The Commission recognizes, however, that the foundation program falls far short of a 'really good' common school education. It believes that the schools of Illinois ultimately provide a program which is genuinely good, rather than essentially mediocre. The Commission's definition of a 'good' education is in terms of practices now found to be successful in Illinois schools that are well organized, well managed, and well financed. The Commission favors a 'really good' education, an education that is distinctly superior to the foundation level, as the ultimate goal for the schools of Illinois. The

Commission supports a superior program of education because it realizes that one of the greatest tasks of education today is to provide an enlightened citizenry able to meet the problems of the times through the effective working of self-government.

On these fundamental issues there must be, and there has been, no partisan division. All of the school commissioners I have selected have been non-political and have functioned without any partisan considerations. I commend for our consideration the words of the President of the United States when he wrote recently to the National Citizens Commission for Public Schools as follows:

The success of our schools in educating our children and youth in the principles of democracy is of basic importance if democracy is to win out over communism. It is just as important for us to provide each child and youth with the education he needs to become a constructive citizen as it is to provide more and better weapons for our defense.

We must be watchful that, in meeting the challenge that has been forced upon us, we do not neglect the education of our children. If that should ever happen, we would be sacrificing a fundamental part of our way of life.

Every good citizen should be concerned in these days with how he can best serve his country. Not the least among the duties of each citizen is to work earnestly and wholeheartedly for better schools in his own community. I urge each member of your organization to continue your efforts in this important task.

DALLAS COUNCIL ON WORLD AFFAIRS
April 23

I SUPPOSE THIS WILL BE known as one of those convulsive periods in human history which witness the death of an old era and the birth of a new. The process is painful and tumultuous, and accompanied by all manner of tension, disorder and torment. The teacher in a grammar school asked the class: "What shape is the earth?" and a small boy quickly answered: "My father says it's in the worst shape it ever was." Perhaps it is. Bernard Shaw once remarked: "If the other planets are inhabited they must be using the earth as their insane asylum."

But, of course, anxiety is nothing new. Long ago, Hezekiah, King of Judah, facing a crisis in Judah's relations with Assyria, said: "This is a day of trouble, and of rebuke, and blasphemy."

We commonly think of the nineteenth century as a calm and hopeful age. Yet in 1806, William Pitt said: "There is scarcely anything around us but ruin and despair." Even the fathers of our Constitution had their bad moments. In 1829, John Randolph of Virginia said: "The country is ruined past redemption."

But all these dire forebodings came to nothing. A look at history from where we sit in the mid-twentieth century, confounded with difficulties and tormented with anxiety, should provide us a little perspective and much hope.

It seems as though the most creative and enterprising periods in human history have always been troubled and disorderly. The sixteenth century witnessed the flowering of the Renaissance, but a great contemporary, Erasmus, called that stirring era "the excrement of the ages." So too the eighteenth century which we regard as one of the most creative, with the American and French Revolutions, was to Rousseau "this great rottenness in which we live."

I take some comfort from the contrast between the historical and contemporary view of violent and disturbed eras. But I take no satisfaction in the current habits of looking for scapegoats to blame for our difficulties—difficulties, anxieties and tensions which are the consequence of our present position of world leadership.

It is correct to say that this country never asked for or explicitly chose its present position. But we are not there because of some person's bad judgment or because of an historical accident. We made the choice unconsciously by making many decisions in our past that resulted in our present greatness. We expanded westward and settled a great continent bordering on two oceans. We developed our country industrially, largely on the basis of an expanding internal market. We developed a government on the principles of consent and accountability that gives us internal political strength. We fought in two wars, hoping to be free of great anxieties at their end, only to find that the power balance was changed by the outcome of the wars—England and France weakened, Germany and Japan eclipsed, the Soviet Union confronting us. We have great responsibilities, not because we wanted them, but because as a nation we made choices in our past that made them inevitable.

Jefferson foresaw this. Writing to John Adams in 1816 he foretold our position of influence and power: "We are destined," he said, "to be a barrier against the return of ignorance and barbarism. "Of our continental strength he wrote: "What a stand will it secure as a ralliance for the reason and freedom of the globe!" He foresaw America assuming leadership: "Old Europe will have to lean on our shoulders . . . and to hobble along by our side " he said.

Now all this has come to pass (and probably come to stay) and it makes us miserable, so we exchange epithets and accusations and look for someone, preferably Democrats, to blame for it all. Instead of acting like Walt Whitman's "resolute breed of men" many of us react more like readers of the "Whodunit" mystery thrillers. That mature people with any historical perspective should feel dismayed and betrayed if there is not perfect efficacy in foreign policy disturbs me. I recall a story told in Mexico. A man heavy in need and great in faith wrote a letter asking for 100 pesos. He addressed it to God and mailed it. The postmaster had no idea how to handle the letter. He opened it, seeking a clue. Touched by the man's story of need, he passed the hat among the postal employees. Thus 75 pesos were raised and placed in an envelope to await the return of the importuning man. A few days later he was back, inquiring for mail. He was given the envelope, opened it counted the money and glowered. Then he went to the counter and painfully wrote out another letter. It read: "Dear God: I am still 25 pesos short. Please make up the difference. But don't send it through the local post office. I think it is full of thieves."

There can be no perfect efficacy in the conduct of foreign affairs and the "Whodunit" approach to world problems will yield no solutions. Actually, the severity of the crisis in which we must, whether we like it or not, play a leading role, is due to a conjunction of separate crises no one of which would in itself have been too formidable but all of which taken together put a fearful burden upon us. Of these separate crises, three, at least, are due to science.

(1) A century of continuous social and economic revolution now reaching full speed largely because of the belief that modern techniques fully applied in peace could give a higher living standard to everyone, ergo, must.

(2) Modern communications and transport that by transforming the entire planet into a single strategical area have made necessary thinking in terms of a world balance of power and increased the difficulty of localizing armed conflicts.

(3) New weapons which, while no more lethal than the flu epidemic, are terrifying by the amount of killing and destruction they can accomplish at one clip—hence awakening greater fear of war.

(4) Basic too, I think, is the decline in the belief in previous fixed values nearly everywhere, thus making it more difficult to appeal to nations and groups to do what is necessary and to recognize dangers in time, while increasing their vulnerability to the new religion of communism.

(5) The head start in territorial and arms expansion seized by the U.S.S.R. while our policy was to disarm unilaterally and try to tempt Stalin into cooperation rather than opposition; and

(6) The apparently uncompromisingly aggressive nature of Soviet Communism.

Obviously, the first four of these would exist if there had never been a U.S.S.R. or if it underwent a drastic change tomorrow. And none of them are going to be spirited away by hysteria or political claptrap to catch unwary voters. I think we know that McCarthyism and loose talk may take the headlines but they won't take the American people.

Foreign policy is now a life and death matter, and anything but honest, straightforward talk borders on treason. Most of us know that our difficulties and frustrations cannot be blamed on any single individual or group. Our troubles as well as our triumphs find their explanation in the full sweep of recent history for which we are all in part responsible. Our international position today is part and parcel of developments that result from actions of whole peoples and groups of peoples over a long period of time.

None of us can glibly toss off a share of responsibility for our present international position. And we won't find the architects of our woes hiding under the bed or sitting in public office.

Common sense tells us that the stuff of history is rich and complex and not within the sure control of any one nation. Our national power is enormous. But there is a lot of other power loose in the world—military power, historic traditions, ethnic loyalties, ideologies. Our position gives us a chance to influence and to beguile world history. But we cannot determine it. New faces in Washington, whoever they are, cannot make everything come out just the way this nation wants it.

Of course we are disappointed that prospects for tranquilty are not brighter. But most of us know that life by its very nature is never free of trouble. Life is not so much getting one's way as working one's way. And I think most of us know that. Beneath the anxious, confused surface of our daily life something deep and sound has been happening. "Whodunit" is an irritable reaction from blithe optimism. Optimism is pleasant but it can never save the nation. It distorts facts, disguises issues, hides perils.

But it seems to me obvious that most Americans, irrespective of party, have a pretty sound outlook on the world and sense how dangerous an antagonist the Soviet Union really is. We were not the first to be attacked. But because of our power and our success this country is the Kremlin's chief concern. The United States is the one great obstacle to a world safe for communism. We are the symbol of hope to all men who aspire to be free and stand erect. Queen Juliana said that what her children remember of New York is their last glimpse of the Statue of Liberty from the deck of the Queen Mary: "A hand sticking out of the fog, holding a torch." America is a torch in the fog, and the Soviet leaders would like to douse the torch.

My impression is that most of us are now also aware of the duplicity of Soviet strategy—the practice of "double diplomacy"—a set of slogans for home consumption, a set of slogans for foreign confusion; warfare against the Russian people, warfare against all foreigners; political and military warfare, simultaneous or interchangeable. Communism speaks with the voice of idealism but has the hand of the cynic. Perhaps its greatest influence springs from the fact that it has made the miserable of the world more conscious of their misery and lures them into dictatorship by the offer of "democracy," into tyranny by the promise of "justice," into servitude by the pledge of "freedom." Yet we know how it inflames the hearts and hopes of the ignorant and needy to whom elocution about democracy is meaningless.

I believe we have made up our minds about another matter. This nation has rejected isolation as the way to security in our shrunken world. Isolation was buried during World War II when we established the United Nations. This was before the full peril of the Soviet threat was clear, but that peril has only reinforced the national decision to go forward with allies. This country has emphatically and definitively concluded, I believe, that the time to stop aggression is before it starts and that the way to do it is by organized action of the community of free people.

We have been engaged for some time in the formidable task of building this community of free peoples—first through the United Nations; then through the North Atlantic Treaty Organization to strengthen the crucial Western European peninsula; simultaneously by developing the important Organization of America States in our own hemisphere and by numerous other treaties, agencies, and policies.

We talk incessantly of our failures and Communist successes but it is well to remember that Communist enroachment was successfully opposed in Greece and Turkey, their blockade in Berlin was met by ingenuity and counter-measures, and their aggression in Korea was battled head on. The prompt and firm response to the North Korean aggression was part and parcel of a strategy of collective security which had been in the making for a long time and which had been urged, welcomed, and agreed upon long since with virtual unanimity by the American people.

Our immediate reaction through the United Nations to the cynical North Korean attack was greeted at the time with the applause of the entire country. The aggression has been stopped and the aggressors driven back across the 38th parallel from whence they came. Yet now, with the armistice negotiations dragging out, possibly until after the elections, we hear ambitious men in search of votes capitalize on every discontent, every prejudice, every credulity; we hear the repeated charge that the Korean war is "Truman's war," that it is a "useless war," that "we stand exactly where we stood three years ago." But what sort of logic is it to argue that because the continuation of the war does not serve our interests, it was futile from the start?

I do not know how soon we can expect an armistice in Korea, or whether there will be an armistice at all. The decision rests with the same Communist leaders who gave the signal for the attack on South Korea. But perhaps never has a more important action received less adequate explanation than the prompt intervention of the United States through the United Nations in Korea. The defense of South Korea was the first time in the world's history that military force was used by an international organization to turn back aggression. While Korea has not proved definitely that collective security will work, it has prevented the Soviet Union from proving that it won't work. And the Korean experience has hastened the development of the General Assembly of the United Nations as an agency for the enforcement of the United Nations' decisions against aggression, free from the Soviet veto.

Korea put the American rearmament effort into high gear. Now our increasing strength both inhibits and puts us in a better position to answer any new Communist aggression.

Also, the strong stand we took on Korea, together with a stepped-up rearmament program, has had an important effect on the morale of the peoples of western Europe and has encouraged them to build up their own defenses. NATO would not have the strength it has today if we had not acted promptly and decisively to support the United Nations in Korea.

Our action in Korea also had valuable results throughout the Far East; it contributed greatly to the successful negotiation of a peace treaty with Japan, and to the conclusion of mutual security treaties with the Philippines, Australia and New Zealand, as well as Japan.

Finally, the Soviet Union now knows that the path of conquest is mortally dangerous. The Korean aggression very likely was planned as merely the first of a series of military actions—initially by satellites, finally to be undertaken by the Soviet Union itself. If so, the lesson of Korea may be of historic importance.

Of course, speculation about possible adjustments in the thinking of the Kremlin must be cautious. Perhaps for a time the Soviet Union will now content itself with maneuvers in the cold war, like wooing Germany from the West; or perhaps Western strength of will is to be further tested by some other military challenge, or even more sternly tested by a peace offensive calculated to retard the rearmament program. We dare not tie our policies to any one assumption regarding Soviet intentions. Whatever those intentions are, however, the Soviet miscalculation in Korea will make them harder of fulfillment, and to call a war launched by Moscow "Truman's war" or a "useless war" is not only misleading but mischievous.

I believe our government has done well in diligently and painfully seeking to limit the war to Korea. We have been concerned not only to frustrate our immediate antagonists, but to use force to avoid a full scale holocaust. For this reason, we have to be patient about the full settlement of the Korean problem. A satisfactory settlement—the unification of Korea as a free nation—is likely to take a long time and to wait upon settlements of other issues. And we may yet fail in our effort to keep the Korean fighting from spreading—the aggressor has a lot to say about that.

There is another matter on which I find wide agreement—the acceptance of the rearmament and military assistance program as a condition of security now, until, negotiating from strength, we can devise the means of co-existence on a tolerable basis with this inscrutable Russian power in the world.

In an earlier period of crisis, when Greece was challenged by Persia, Heraclitus said: "We have to defend our walls and our laws." So do we and I suspect, thanks in large part to the impetus of Korea, that we are rapidly redressing the balance of power in the world. But certainly the Korean experience as a warning of the possibility of war any time and anywhere must remain in our calculations. The path of Soviet conquest must, until reason can prevail and disarmament safely commence, continue to be mortally dangerous as it was in Korea. Better to pay large insurance premiums than to rebuild the house after a terrible fire.

What is at stake between the free world and the Russians is primarily the decision as to who is going to decide the basis on which the social, economic and political problems of the world are going to be handled. The Soviet Union offers one method, we offer another. I am confident the American people intend to make sure that our democratic experiment will outlast the Soviet system on its merits if we are fortunate enough to face chiefly that test. Marxist doctrine includes the expectation that the capitalist world will one day weaken and destroy itself, largely by its own inner contradictions. But in spite of our predilection for solving problems quickly and putting them behind us, I suspect we could do very well in a waiting contest. Americans are learning to live with some of their problems and we could become as effective in the cold war as we have always asked our military men to be in a hot war.

Each problem of our foreign policy must be tackled soberly, patiently, firmly, in the light of the total situation. We should refuse to be pushed into what looks like a brave policy before we are sure it is not a foolish one. That hard-headed activist, Winston Churchill, once wrote: "Those who are prone by temperament and character, to seek sharp and clear-cut solutions of difficult and obscure problems, who are ready to fight whenever some challenge comes from a foreign power, have not always been right. How many wars have been averted by patience and persisting good will."

No greater difficulty confronts us than the wise and thrifty allocation of our limited resources and capabilities in relation to all the demands upon us. We also have much to learn about how to talk and act with increasing relevance to the problems of the underdeveloped areas and the uncommitted peoples who stand so high on the Kremlin's list. There are ways to increase the brittleness of the Soviet and satellite system; we must find and exploit them.

Crucial to success is our ability to work with our allies. Let us not underestimate this undertaking. And likewise let us not underestimate the difficulty Stalin confronts with alliances maintained by ruthless central leadership. We, on the other hand, must rely on willing allies, drawn to us by a recognition of mutual interests and by confidence in our leadership. There still seem to be some Americans who think we can get along without allies. They admit that our interests and responsibilities are world wide but they prefer to "go it alone," or assume we can pick up the necessary allies at the last moment. They seem to resent efforts to win allies in advance of trouble by mutual agreement to help each other, such as the Atlantic Pact. They somehow expect to have friends without being one. In some ways this brand of isolationism is more dangerous than the old fashioned variety. America First argued we should leave the world alone, overlooking the fact that the world would not leave us alone. The ghost of America First asks us to assume world responsibilities but then advocates policies that would lose us our allies one by one.

Power attracts allies. But the whole tone and style in which we use our power is of primary importance. For power also repels. The nations we must count upon for help in a successful military defense and a promising political advance are weaker than we are. Some of these weaker nations, once alarmed at our isolation, are now worrying about how we will use our power. We should not be too surprised at this. A position of preponderant influence makes us the target of suspicion and criticism. We must admit there are some pretty headstrong people in our midst. Long ago, Ralph Waldo Emerson said: "Beware of the American peacock." Some of our allies are not completely convinced that along with our power and wealth we also know everything about leading a world-wide alliance. But we can show by what we do and say that we do not simply consult our own interests and views but give consideration to the concerns of our allies; that we in truth "have a decent respect for the opinions of mankind." I believe the eagle, and neither the ostrich nor the peacock, will continue to be the American emblem!

This is a dangerous time but it is also an exhilarating one! Indeed, we all must have moments when we feel it is a little too exhilarating! But we can still understand what that editor, about to be beheaded in the French Revolution meant when he said: "It is too bad to take my head off. I wanted to see how all this is coming out."

Let's keep our heads. And it isn't always easy, particulary in an election year—and even if you are not running for office! We've come a long way from the myopic era that followed the First World War. The past is bright with promise for the future. And it is to the future we must look for more permanent and tolerable solutions than the present improvisations. As our muscles harden will the Soviet sue for peace—permanent, secure peace? We can't assume that and there is little evidence for it. Is the hope then to devise means of co-existence with this ruthless and equal power in the world? How to co-exist with evil without becoming evil? How long can we dissipate our national resources? How long can we endure such defense expenditures without fulfilling Marx's prophecy? Are the ultimate destinations, as Senator McMahon asked, military safety at the price of economic disaster, or economic safety at the price of military disaster? And pray heaven we don't develop a fear psychosis about peace and a vested interest in not making peace for fear of economic collapse. How long can we furnish dollars to buy our goods; with no East-West trade across the iron curtain don't we have to face, and soon, creating markets for their goods so they can buy ours?

So, with all the difficulties that are behind us there are still more ahead. But one thing seems certain: We cannot accept as everlasting this era of staggering taxes, towering budgets, and falling dollars. We cannot permit the perpetual concentration of our economy, our resources, our government, our very lives, on the relentless requirements of the arms race. We cannot allow America to become a permanent armed camp forever under the dark shadow of catastrophic war.

Our arms and alliances have purchased us some time, but can they purchase lasting peace? As Tallyrand said: "You can do anything with bayonets except sit on them."

We must try to put an end to the arms race before it puts an end to us. Having at long and painful last redressed the balance of power, buttressed our allies and restored an uneasy stability to the world, we must then push ahead with positive policies to create—out of a political science as imaginative and unprecedented as our military science—a policy of peace to match our present policy of power. Failure to do so would be unforgiveable and unforgotten—if man survived our folly to remember.

This policy of peace must offer us realistic hope that we can halt communist imperialism without appeasement and the arms race without war. The arms race cannot be halted on the basis of pledges and paper promises. We cannot depend upon mere treaties—as we did at the Disarmament Conference of the 1920's and as we did in the Kellog-Briand Pact. We have found since World War II that the signature of the Soviet is not significant.

The arms race can be halted only on the basis of foolproof, enforceable guarantees that no nation, once it has laid down its arms, will be permitted to take them up once again. The United States, of course, has called for disarmament. So has the Soviet government, on impossible terms. I don't know whether a satisfactory foolproof method can be devised which the Russians would accept. But I do know that negotiation will be easier when power is more even and that an everlasting arms race is folly for them as it is for us. And I know that it is worth pursuing with all the intensity and purposefulness that we set out after armaments.

To the miserable millions of Africa and Asia—tempted in their desperation by the false promises of communism—our determination to explore to the end this basic condition of peace and a better world would carry a vision of a day when the resources of the world could be turned from the destruction of war to the construction of peace.

I have mentioned but some of the obstacles and perils that will still beset our path for years to come. One by one they will be met and can be mastered—not by star gazing, not by vaporous yearnings for the dear, dead past, not by second guessing, "whodunit," or the painless prescriptions of political medicine men, but by the same patient, practical wisdom and persistence that has served us so well at home in promoting liberty, establishing justice and ensuring domestic tranquility.

I am reminded of Robert Frost's Vermont farmer—or maybe he was a Texas rancher. When they told him to hitch his wagon to the star, he said: "I'll hitch my wagon to a horse; For I've promises to keep And miles to go before I sleep."

OREGON DEMOCRATIC STATE COMMITTEE JEFFERSON-JACKSON DINNER, PORTLAND
May 1

AT THE TIME YOU invited me, you may have thought you were getting a candidate for President. Instead all you got was a candidate for Governor of Illinois. I hope you don't feel yourselves deceived and defrauded. For my part, I feel a little like the old Confederate soldier, unarmed, ragged and asleep, whom some zealous young soldiers captured. "Get up, Reb, we got you," they shouted. "Yeh," the weary old fellow mumbled, "and it's a heck of a git you got."

But if you have a complaint, so have I! My name is on the Oregon ballot for President in your primary election on May 16. While I am grateful for this friendly and flattering gesture and the good will which prompted it, I wish to make it emphatically clear that my name is not on your primary ballot at my request or with my knowledge or consent. Indeed, I did my best to withdraw, only to discover that under your laws the door was locked and I could not get out.

In the circumstances, all I can do is to request that there be no campaign on my behalf and that the Oregon voters disregard my name on the ballot. Let me repeat that I am a candidate for Governor of Illinois and nothing else. I don't believe a man can, in good conscience, run for two offices at the same time. What's more, I think a man, even a politician, should keep his commitments, and my prior commitment was to run for Governor.

Now, of course, if there happens to be within the range of my voice any Democrat eligible to vote in Illinois I hope he will vote for me—for Governor—and if that calls for an absentee ballot I'll help him get one!

In 1947 I visited the Gifford Pinchot National Forest across the Columbia River in the State of Washington. This forest was so named, you will recall, by order of President Truman, to perpetuate the name of the man who pioneered our national forest system during the administration of Theodore Roosevelt. And that illustrates again, incidentally, that we Democrats and the more progressive Republicans have always been sort of kissin' cousins.

When I visited that beautiful National Forest I was reminded on all sides that many Americans have almost forgotten the Civilian Conservation Corps; how it took hungry, hopeless, homeless boys off metropolitan streets and alleys and put them to useful work. Many were brought here to the inspiring uplands of the Northwest, and many remained to become stalwart citizens. The recreational life of this region is richer today, and will be enriched for a long time to come, by the productive labor of the CCC during the ugly days of the Depression. History will surely record that those difficult years, when the nation was lifted by its bootstraps from the depths of despair largely by the courage and vision of a great champion of the people, were among the finest hours in the long record of Democratic leadership.

But it is not my purpose to talk here about the Depression, ten-cent corn and Herbert Hoover, and all the convenient but threadbare political whipping posts. Rather it seems to me worth while to take a longer look into the past. As party men I think it is well for us not just to do or die, but to reason why.

In the long span of time from Thomas Jefferson to Harry Truman, why is it that the American people have turned most often to the Democratic party for national leadership? Why have we Democrats had the people's confidence the bulk of the time? Why latterly, in this dramatic century, has our destiny been directed most conspicuously by Democrats, from Woodrow Wilson to the present day?

The answer, of course, is compounded of successes and failures by both parties, but on balance the Democratic party has met the people's needs more often than the Republican party and its Federalist and Whig predecessors.

The Republicans found a great principle in the Civil War—national union and human freedom. Afterwards they embraced the principle that what was good for business was good for the nation. Business was protected by tariffs and from cut-throat domestic competition. They passed the Homestead Act, distributed free land, and pensions to soldiers. The era of development was on and they won election after election. What could you do with a party that had emancipated the slaves, saved the union, given everybody a bounty in land or tariff, assured businessmen of prosperity and poor men of a full dinner pail?

But by the turn of our century the Republican party had lost its bearings. It had made its choice and cast its lot with money, big business and the employer. There was no place at the table for the farmer who had to buy in a protected market and sell in a free market. One by one the Republican party deserted the farmer, the working man, the small business man. They deserted the people and at last the people deserted them.

Then came Woodrow Wilson and the New Freedom, Franklin Roosevelt and the New Deal, Harry Truman and the Fair Deal, and through them all runs the long, strong cord of faith in the Jacksonian-Jeffersonian principle that in a people's government the people are sovereign; that our strength and well being don't trickle down from an overflowing cup at the top, but rise up the mighty trunk from the myriad roots that are the people.

I don't know what the present Republican leaders are for and the only thing I'm sure they're against is Democrats. Divided and leaderless, bereft of common purpose, policy, principles or program for the nation and the world, they have only a common name—Republican—and behind it lies deep and bitter conflict and confusion.

I don't know what direction the Republican party is going to take. At the moment it reminds me of the mule who starved to death standing between two stacks of hay trying to make up its mind which to eat.

Torn with irreconcilable conflicts between men and issues, between a vaporous yearning to retreat to a dear, dead past, and the urge to restate and re-assert the great liberal principles of its birth; rudderless between forthright conservatism, hopeless reaction and flattering "me-tooism," the people have said to the once great, proud party of Abraham Lincoln and Theodore Roosevelt, over and over again, in the words of the Book of Revelations: "I know thy works, that thou are neither cold nor hot; I would thou wert cold or hot. So then because thou art lukewarm, and neither cold nor hot, I will spew thee out of my mouth."

They've tried almost everything in the political book. In the Roosevelt days, you will recall, we were belabored with dire prophecies of dictatorship — but the people still rule, and how! Then they said what the Democrats have done is good, but we can do it better. That didn't work either. In President Truman's time they say the administration is too weak—but it was no weak man that called Stalin's hand every time from Greece and Turkey to Korea. Inflation is blamed on the Democrats, but Republicans fight controls. War is blamed on the Democrats, but some Republicans that never fade away clamor for bigger, hotter wars. Spending is blamed on the Democrats but Republicans join in droves to override President Truman's veto of an unprecedented pension grab. While condoning character assassination and fake photographs linking Senator Tydings and Earl Browder they shamelessly prate of morals and decency in public life. Because the administration has thrown Russian expansion onto the defensive, Republicans applaud careless inquisitions and irresponsible accusations of treachery.

It is sad that America, at the height of her power, influence and well-being, should be ringing with slander, epithet, ill temper and the counsels of political desperation when all the world looks to us for dignity, sanity and confident leadership.

But the people have been listening to these voices for the last twenty years now, ever since they prophesied that grass would grow in the streets of America, and meanwhile we have emerged from grim depression and never been more prosperous; we have destroyed the Nazi menace and are fighting the even greater Communist menace to a standstill with words, weapons and the faith of free men.

But by no means all Republicans have capitulated to this shadow of fear and mistrust that slopes across our bright land. I wish these things could be said of none of them. Yes, and I wish all of us Democrats were spotless, and blameless, because there is much more at stake in all this current orgy of epithet and injury than the welfare of any man or, indeed, the result of any election.

Long ago the first Republican uttered some words which reckless politicians would well ponder. Abraham Lincoln said: "In times like the present, men should utter nothing for which they would not willingly be responsible through time and eternity."

And I might add that not only should we say nothing, but do nothing for which we would not wish to be held accountable in the future. The responsibility for our moral standards rests heaviest upon the men and women in public life, because public confidence in the integrity of the government is indispensable to faith in democracy.

And I am proud that Democrats in both houses of Congress have led the battle to expose corruption and corrupt officials. Let there be no misunderstanding; as Democrats, proud of our party and its long record of service and leadership, we have not, we do not, and we will not condone, excuse or explain away wrongdoing or moral obliquity in public office, whoever the guilty and whatever their station.

While we know that it is "we the people" who corrupt officials, we also know that one corrupt official is one too many, just as one corrupt private citizen is one too many. A dishonest official is as faithless to his party as he is to his office, and the party of Jefferson and Jackson must never founder on the rocks of moral equivocation.

I am reminded of words Charles Evans Hughes used while speaking of the great Republican scandals that followed the First World War: "Neither political party has a monopoly of virtue or of rascality. Let wrong be exposed and punished, but let no partisan Pecksniffs affect a 'holier than thou' attitude. Guilt is personal and knows no party."

To that I say "amen." If there is Democratic dirt, then let us clean it up and turn the flashlight into every dark corner. But we will not blush for the Democratic record of probity and honor and fidelity to public trust during twenty long years and the vast multiplication of the hazard of dishonesty and betrayal.

While the faithless must be exposed and rooted out of every place of public trust, it will be a tragic disaster if we forget the tens of thousands of honest, conscientious public servants. Generalities about crime and corruption in government which embrace the many good with the few bad can only make it harder to induce good people to enter public service. We do not lose faith in the banking system because a few bankers turn out to be embezzlers.

For the information of the public and the morale of the multitude of decent, faithful men and women on whom government depends, I think it just as important to recognize and support the good as it is to find and punish the bad.

And we have also witnessed the stifling, choking effect of witch hunting, the paralysis of initiative, the discouragement and intimidation that follow in its wake and inhibits the bold, imaginative thought and discussion that is the anvil of policy. Pray heaven that reckless partisanship and political expediency in connection with the grafters and opportunists that foul our nest do not follow the same part of extremism and further weaken the fabric of our public life.

Let's don't throw out the baby with the bath! Let's don't burn down the barn to roast the pig!

The Democratic party has been in power for twenty years. Of course, you don't fire a man who is doing a good job just because he has done it for a long time. But it is not enough in this campaign year just to point to the spectacular achievements of these two great decades. The Democratic party must give the American people conclusive reasons for continuing in power. Nor can we achieve this great end with but a small risk. We must not try to persuade the public and ourselves that there are easy solutions to the hard problems which confront the United States. We must not represent as simple what is infinitely complex, or represent as safe what is infinitely precarious.

The twenty years during which we have governed the United States was a period of change as rapid and violent as any in history. The forces that demanded change shattered many societies. We contained them within the American system of democratic government, popular control, and civil liberty. There has been no break in the continuity of our institutions: the United States has held to the course of development which it has been following for a hundred and fifty years. The party that achieved this triumph of stability in a time of world revolution did not do so by pretending that there were short cuts to safety, prosperity, freedom, or social justice, or that they could be bought at a discount. It must not minimize the difficulties or the dangers now.

During those two decades the United States rose to the pinnacle of world power. No nation ever reached such a position with so little premeditation—or so reluctantly. Vestiges of our reluctance still cling to us like bits of a chrysalis—a recurrent inability to realize how great our strength is, impulses to ignore its implications, impulses to avoid the responsibilities it has created. But these hesitations are rather the necessarily deliberate functioning of democratic institutions than evidence of unsteady purpose. We have not failed to act with confidence and courage. The decision to rearm, the decision to ally ourselves with the free nations of Europe, the North Atlantic treaty, the Marshall Plan, the Berlin air-lift, Greece and Turkey, the acceptance of the Communist challenge to the free world in Korea—these were the acts of a great nation accepting the full responsibility of its power.

In the years ahead the United States will be called on repeatedly to act with the same courage and decision. We have had to take the largest part in building the piers and abutments for mankind's bridge to a peaceful world. We know that we must take the largest part in building the bridge. That fact dominates all others today, and it is so hard a fact that there is a terrible urgency to shrink from it. In an election year we might be tempted to represent it as less dangerous than it is, as calling for less effort and less sacrifice than it does.

We know that our opponents will try to soften the hard fact. The Republican party will offer the American people the mirage of a security that is not possible in the world today. It will continue to use the two instruments of illusion which nothing yet has been able to strike from its hands. One is nostalgia for an era that can never be brought back, a dream of turning history's clock back to a time when the world was simpler and the United States less powerful. The other is fear—fear of what may happen if we accept the leadership from which in fact there can be no escape.

We know that cry of nostalgia and fear. It says that the world is less harsh than we know it is. In the same breath it says the world is so harsh that only retreat from it can save us. And it adds that if such panic does not save us quite enough, there must be ways of buying safety with half-measures or at half price.

The Democratic party repudiates the illusion. It bids the United States seek safety in realities. They are hard and stern but an adult nation will hold by them. We must build securely on the foundation we have erected. We must go always farther, buttressing and enlarging the position which, with the free nations, we have occupied. We accept risk and danger as terms given. The answer is vigilance, strain, steady nerves, the resolution to endure—and no man dares predict the end. But thus we seize the initiative, act positively, and focus our greatest strength on the weakness at the core of absolutism that must eventually destroy it. We stand on what the American experience has proved many times, that freedom is power, and that freedom breeds freedom. There is no place where it will not fight for us so long as we act in awareness of our strength. Even at this moment it fights for us behind the Iron Curtain, a fifth column which no terrorism can root out—the will of slaves to be free.

The current of domestic change has been no less rapid in these twenty years. It has been attended by many dangers, and it still is. Historically, the Democratic party has been the instrument with which the American people have effected by evolutionary stages, the changes necessary to keep their society in healthy equilibrium. We boast that we are the party of the people—and we must continue to make good the boast.

The everlasting danger of a people's party is that it may become a party of groups. Especially in an election year there are temptations to enhance political power by manipulating and exalting the powers of groups. The people are all the people, and a party which tries to buy, to bribe a group is bargaining to sell the people out. We should betray our tradition if we should fail to direct the power of government against any concentration of group power that had grown too great for a healthy equilibrium. The Democratic party is no man's party; it is every man's party. It must never become a labor party, a farmer party or the party of any group. That would be disaster for the party and disaster for the group. Labor, agriculture, industry, business, minorities, the military—none of them can be allowed a vested interest against the people as a whole. The function of the people's party is to make sure there is a rightful and healthy equilibrium among them all.

And we must realize that government itself may become too great a concentration of power, that indeed a constant tendency of all governments is to accumulate power, and that this tendency must be resisted. So great is the complexity of society today, so intricate its interrelationships, so difficult the job of supervision and administration, that the national government has and must have far more and far greater powers than was required when the world was simpler.

We are caught between the millstones. In a world of big business, big industry, and big labor and big enemies, there must be big government too, and yet it remains true that the least government, the least possible, is the best government. This dilemma would be a matter for despair, if the nature of our federal republic did not contain the means of resolving it. The check against concentration of federal power is the effective functioning of state and local governments. Indeed, a prime cause of the centralization of power in Washington has been the failure of local governments. I think it would be more profitable if we talked less of states' rights and more of states' wrongs—the failure to perform necessary functions adequately at the local level. The tradition of the Democratic party is vigorous home rule. So we Democrats must dedicate ourselves to the reinvigoration of local government.

Just one more word about the most important matter of all.

I believe the people of both parties know that the great unfinished business of our generation and our party is peace. Not war, but peace. They know that victory in this day and age is no longer a condition, but only a word, that with each successive war and each successive victory the problems of peace do not diminish, they multiply. And they know that there is no safety for America in solitude. They know we can't go it alone. They know there is no short cut to the great goal. They know better, I suspect, than shallow politicians that there is only one way—the slow, patient, steadfast, hard way.

In the black night of World War II, how many of us looked back on the lost Thirties and wished that the free world had stopped Fascist aggression in its tracks? We mourned Japanese aggression in Manchuria, the Mussolini adventures in Ethiopia, and Hitler's ravaging of the Rhineland and then the Sudetenland. And we wished that the sage advice of Henry Stimson and Franklin Roosevelt and Winston Churchill had been heeded.

Aggression piled on aggression until all of us were involved.

But in Korea, cynical, calculated Communist aggression was met head on, and stopped! The aggressors have been driven back across the 38th parallel, whence they came. Yet now, with the armistice negotiations dragging out, perhaps until after the elections, we hear ambitious men in search of votes capitalize on every discontent, every prejudice, every credulity. We hear the repeated charge that the Korean war is "Truman's war," that it is a "useless war" and that "we stand exactly where we stood three years ago."

But I ask you this: what sort of logic is it to argue that because the continuation of the war does not serve our interests, it was futile from the start? If the Republican party had won the election of 1948, would we have sat supinely by? The record shows that Governor Dewey's voice was among the many raised in support of the firm and prompt response of the free world to the Communist assault in Korea. And that response was part and parcel of a strategy of collective security which had been in the making a long time and which had been urged, welcomed, and agreed upon long since by the American people. To call this historic first combined resistance to aggression; to call this first effort to make the principle of collective security work for the sake of peace on earth, Truman's war, is both misleading and mischievous.

I do not know how soon we may expect an armistice in Korea, or whether there will be an armistice at all. The decision rests with the same Communist leaders who gave the signal for the original attack. But I believe our government has done well in diligently and painfully seeking to limit the war to Korea. We must not be trapped or pushed into what looks like a brave policy before we are sure it is not a foolish one. As Winston Churchill once said: "Many wars have been averted by patience and persistent good will."

We Americans have a predilection for solving problems quickly and putting them behind us. But we are learning rapidly that we are engaged in what may be a long test of staying power between the free world and Communism, to determine who is going to decide the basis on which the social, economic and political problems of the world are going to be handled.

There are, of course, some Republican leaders like your own Senator Morse, and like Governor Warren, and many in the rank and file, whose philosophy seems to differ little from our own, who share our conviction that government in this age has a responsibility for the economic as well as the physical welfare of the people, and who understand the role of world leadership which has—whether we like it or not—been thrust upon us.

Our strength and the strength of America lies in the many who talk little and think much on this disordered world; the many who know that there are no painless solutions to war, inflation, communism, imperialism, hunger, fear, intolerance and all the hard, stubborn problems that beset us. The perils and obstacles that beset our path will be met, and can be mastered—not by star-gazing, not by second guessing, not by nostalgic yearnings for a simpler but dead past, not by the nostrums of political medicine men, but by the same patient, practical wisdom and persistence that have served us so long and so well in promoting liberty, establishing justice and insuring domestic tranquility all across our nation's and our party's history.

Perhaps it isn't the right thing to say at a party gathering, but who wins or loses the next election is less important than what wins: what ideas, what concept of the world of tomorrow, what quality of perception, leadership and courage. Will we stand fast and pay the price, whatever it be, for freedom? Or will the counsels of fear, of retreat, of isolation prevail?

These are questions that will be answered next November. The days of decision are upon us. Time is running out.

I hope and pray that the people will decide wisely and decisively. I hope and pray that the campaign will be conducted with a dignity and a restraint befitting the solemnity of the issues. For whatever we sow, we shall reap. And no man, no party, no nation can long escape that inexorable law of life. As Americans first and Democrats second, we have more than a selfish reason to remember it.

NATIONAL CONFERENCE OF SOCIAL WORK, CHICAGO
May 26

WHEN I WAS FIRST ASKED to come here tonight I didn't realize I was being accorded an opportunity that very few of my predecessors as governor of Illinois have enjoyed. I wasn't aware until recently that this is the first time since 1893 that the National Conference of Social Work has met in Illinois. That was the year of the first Chicago World's Fair, and it was a long time ago. It was a long time before I was born, and probably before some of you were born too!

Of course we are delighted to have you now, and in such large numbers after such a long absence But candor compels me to say that we feel just a little neglected and hurt that you have stayed away so long. I hope your long absence does not mean that you thought us in some way inhospitable in 1893. I refuse to believe that you thought Chicago offered, in this long interval, no attraction comparable to "Little Egypt" of the first World's Fair. Sally Rand would hate me for even suggesting that possibility. I prefer to think that you looked upon Illinois as such a socially enlightened state that the beneficent influences of your conference was not needed here and could be better applied elsewhere.

Whatever the reason for your long absence, we are sincerely happy to have you back and I hope very much that you are made to feel so welcome that you will want to return soon—and often.

We speak with pride of the social services this state has offered to its citizens through the years. More than a century ago Dorothea Linn Dix aroused the governor and the legislature over the tragic plight of the mentally ill and in 1839 there was established in Jacksonville what was than called a "hospital for the insane." A few years later, in 1848, Samuel Bacon came out of the East and established in the same city a school for blind children. This promptly became a state-supported school. Both of these institutions have served all through the years and have helped to pioneer in new fields of service to the mentally ill and the sightless.

In 1879 this conference met in Chicago for the first time. The then governor of Illinois, Shelby M. Cullom, spoke to the conference and told the members:

> As a state, Illinois claims to stand in the very front rank of civilized communities in respect to the enforcement of law, the punishment of crime, and the care of the diseased and unfortunate. But I have long thought, and am more strongly impressed with the idea since I have been personally connected with the administration of our public institutions, that we have hardly made a beginning in the direction of the reform of criminals and the prevention of crime.
>
> We punish crime, and by its punishment gain much for the peace and security of society in the deterrent influence of punishment; but too large a percentage of those discharged from our penal institutions go directly back to vicious associations and criminal practices. Too many convicts are serving a second and third term in our penitentiaries to warrant the claim that they are, to all, places of penitence and reform."

Governor Cullom's words of more than eighty years ago still could be applied, with more than a little truth, today. Of course we have made substantial progress in penal administration and in parole methods, but the basic problems of prevention of crime and dependency—the fundamental problem of finding permanent solutions rather than temporary cures, is exactly the same today as it was then.

Consider briefly the history of philanthropic enterprise in America.

In the beginning all philanthropy was private. The money poured out by the first families of philanthropy went with warm emotional intent into the organization of new movements, the creation of new agencies, the development and maintenance of new services for the underprivileged. Visiting nursing agencies, hospitals and clinics, anti-tuberculosis societies, settlements, charitable societies and character-building agencies, were sponsored and heavily financed by humanitarian minded people of substantial wealth.

These were the pioneering days of philanthropic leadership. Those days ended about thirty years ago. In the past quarter century the governmental systems of public health, public welfare and public assistance have come into being to provide a floor of basic services supported by everyone through public funds. During this period we recognized that social welfare involved public responsibility.

At the same time, there developed modern community-wide campaign methods to systematically broaden the base of private philanthropy—to reach into everybody's pockets for the support of the voluntary charitable agencies. Measured in money costs, the expansion of both public and private services in these fields in the past three decades has been almost astronomical. In broad terms no one can doubt that the result is a positive contribution to a better way of American life.

But the great systems of public and private service are now exhibiting a serious weakness. Their very size forces their leaders to concentrate upon the maintenance of activities to which they are traditionally committed. Ambitions for expansion express themselves in promoting customary patterns, rather than in new creative directions, or in a search for solutions of basic causes of dependency. Increasing competition for the tax dollar, and the voluntary dollar, compels greater attention to promotion and to public relations. The preoccupation of leadership tends to be with the support of activities rather than with preventing the necessity for them; with digging trenches for a holding action instead of marshaling resources for community-wide attack.

The real heart of the matter is that few of our major public systems or national private movements now devote any substantial portion of their leadership or money, to creative, objective and systematic thought and research into methods of reducing the area of welfare needs. This is the functional weakness which, in my opinion, offers a new kind of challenge to the modern philanthropist—individual or corporate. We do not need new agencies—in fact many people believe we have too many already. Neither are we in need of investment of large sums of money in new types of service. What is needed is the investment of relatively small amounts of money in strategic locations that will result in the improvement and the better coordination of the service that we now have.

It is not surprising that public welfare services, as we now know them, have grown so fast. We must remember that public welfare was born in the depression-cursed Thirties when literally hundreds of thousands of citizens were unemployed and without the basic necessities of life.

Public welfare, in that emergency, was born practically full grown. It had to be established in a hurry and on a big scale, for public welfare became overnight, and still is, big business. We have only to remember that at one time during the Depression nearly twenty-five percent of the families in this country were receiving some kind of governmental aid to realize why public welfare became a vital public obligation. There are still more than five million cases of public assistance in this country at an annual cost of about $2,250,000,000.

Therefore, this new business, manned by many people with very little past experience to go on, has been preoccupied mainly with matters of administrative methods and control—with problems of budget and finance, and with the uncertainties of its relationship to the public. Most of the people within the public welfare movement have had no time to look up from their work and think about the nature of their tasks and the community setting in which they operate.

Opportunity for that kind of thinking has now become a critical necessity. Some people wonder why, after more than ten years of full employment we have as many people as we do still on relief and at such great cost. Administrators of public aid can cite various reasons for this in general terms, but we do not know ourselves nearly as much as we would like to know about why they are there, and why more of these dependents cannot be self-sustaining.

And so I say it is time that we gave more attention to dependency as a problem to be solved, instead of looking upon it primarily as a condition which affords good reason for giving people the money they must have to maintain a decent living.

I am glad to note that the need for this greater concentration on causes and solutions rather than methods is gaining some recognition. Government and some private agencies are beginning to see that more money and more building is not the ultimate answer to our needs. We are doing some of this research here in Illinois, as for example in our new hospital at Galesburg where we are studying the problems of the aging, and in our new research center for treatment of very young mentally ill at Peoria. Some of the private agencies are carrying on community-wide studies looking toward possible reductions in welfare costs. There should and doubtless will be more of this.

It is really not my intention here to pose as an expert in a field in which you have had much broader experience than I. But as one who comes into frequent contact with these problems you face every day, I feel that I am somewhat familiar with your basic difficulties and I hope you will permit me to offer another bit of gratuitous advice.

I don't need to tell you that every year reams of paper and millions of words are used to criticize the operations of public and private welfare services. The criticism is far more vigorous and frequent than the praise. Usually this criticism deals with frauds or alleged extravagance in public assistance. Publicity usually is given to an isolated case or cases, of fraud or administrative failure, and the result is to create the public impression that fraud is rampant. People are given the idea that because there are occasional cases of chiseling, the whole program is mismanaged.

That is a dangerous condition. The only effective way to deal with it is through stronger administration and case supervision. Careful, meticulous management of the distribution of public funds, and of those funds contributed by the voluntary agencies, is absolutely essential to the development of the public confidence that is so important.

We have tried hard in Illinois to eliminate the chiselers from the public assistance rolls by establishing a separate frauds investigation branch in the Illinois Public Aid Commission. We have made definite strides in eliminating evils and abuses, and the results have been apparent in declining public assistance rolls in this state. There has been a steady decline in the number of recipients under most of the public aid catagories and actual expenditures of the IPAC have been running about a million dollars per month less than budget estimates.

In that connection you may be interested to know what Illinois' experience has been in the operation of the state law enacted in 1951 eliminating secrecy in public assistance rolls.

That law became operative last November. Each month since then the Illinois Public Aid Commission has posted lists of recipients in county welfare departments in all of the 102 counties of the state. These lists contain names and amounts paid in monthly allowances under the old age pension, aid to dependent children, blind and disability insurance and general relief.

Opposition to opening the rolls to the public had been based chiefly on the contention that recipients would be humiliated by malicious gossip, and that the rolls would be utilized for wrongful purposes.

The commission has reported publicly in recent weeks that experience has proved both of these fears to be groundless. The law in Illinois requires the person requesting to examine rolls, to sign his name and state the purpose of his request. By actual count, only 192 persons asked to inspect the rolls in all of the 102 counties between Nov. 2 and April 1, or an average of less than two per county in five months. Eighty-three of these requests came in the first month, mostly from newspapers checking on rumors that large numbers of ineligibles were on the relief rolls. They found the rumors were without basis in fact and significantly, newspaper requests have been negligible since the first lists were posted.

Other requests came from private welfare agencies, from school officials, from aid recipients who wanted to see if they were listed for the sums they actually were receiving, and so forth. The requests indicated a proper motive in every instance, according to the commission. Its report added that while the number of requests to examine the lists had been small the elimination of secrecy actually had been beneficial in two important respect:

First, it has helped to scotch irresponsible rumors that relief rolls were loaded with persons undeserving of public assistance, and

Second, it has deterred some persons of likely or certain ineligibility from trying to get on the relief or assistance rolls.

I suspect it is entirely too soon to speak with confidence that the fears expressed about this legislation are baseless, but certainly thus far our Illinois experience has apparently been less harmful than beneficial.

Public information in the whole welfare field seems to me one of our greatest deficiencies. Like so much that relates to government and public administration, orderly, well managed welfare work attracts little attention. Only mismanagement, scandal and fraud seem to be newsworthy. But I am not one of those who believe that "there is no truth in the news and there is no news in the truth." So I would urge you to look for opportunities for frequent and full interpretation of the work you are doing, and the methods you are applying in your respective communities to these same ends. Generally I believe the newspapers will be receptive and helpful if they are convinced that they are being given the full story, and not what we conveniently call propaganda. I suggest that you enlist their help in intelligent efforts to improve your public relations, in increasing public understanding of the tremendous administrative tasks many of you face from day to day.

I would suggest further that your agencies should look for opportunities to utilize also the radio and television and other media of mass communication to present your story—in general, to take the people into your confidence. I think these methods will prove to be much more effective than expensive brochures or forbidding statistical reports which few people read, especially the people you are trying to reach. In fact, I am convinced that these elaborate and expensive publications sometimes add to confusion and misunderstanding rather than dispel it.

One further word before I sit down. I'd like to make an observation on another phase of your work that no doubt has occurred to many of you with increasing emphasis in the last few years. That is the relationship between our activities in the whole field of public welfare, and our nation's new responsibilities of leadership in world affairs.

We live in an age of strange contradictions. The first half of this century has produced many moral, social, and scientific advances. At the same time, it has produced a great depression and two world wars, and even now we may be perilously close to a third. The same age that has seen science produce every sort of material comfort and convenience has also seen atomic energy harnessed, not to constructive purposes, but largely to those of mass destruction.

In the light of the grim realities of these days two facts stand out with clarity: the obvious need for strong and progressive welfare services available to citizens who really need them, and the possibility that there may be less money to carry on these activities. Every citizen today, every business, every interest, knows that we are engaged in a struggle for survival, and that this is and must be the paramount concern of all of us. A struggle of this sort involves a vast preparedness program, the cost of which could easily do permanent damage to a free economy. We are going to have to tighten our belts. It is better that we do this deliberately and voluntarily than in the haste of necessity and involuntarily.

At the same time, in this hour of trial, every lost soul that could have been salvaged is a blot upon our record and a liability as well. Today we perceive again our need for robust manpower, men and women with the physical and emotional stamina to meet the rigors of military service and to perform all of the tasks of an expanded defense program. Just as tanks and planes cannot be built overnight, neither can we build overnight mentally and physically healthy men and women.

How can we reconcile these two necessities? In the light of both of them I think we must pause and re-examine the total welfare picture and ask ourselves: where are we going? If we must tighten our belts and put first things first in the welfare field, as I think we must, we had best do it intelligently with a long-range overall plan, not by improvisation and patchwork.

As the most prosperous democratic nation on earth we have far more to contribute to other nations than our dollars, and the best contribution we can make is through example. This country, for so long youthful and ambitious, has reached its maturity. The world needs our leadership, not only in the military sense and the ideological sense, but also our experience in human relations.

What we have done in developing insurance, public assistance, and institutional care, are examples. We borrowed some of these ideas from older nations. We have developed and improved upon many of them. Our financial strength has permitted us to raise standards and to better train professional leadership. In the medical sciences and technology we have added to the strength of man and his comfort. We have also developed better relations among men, with an understanding of the right of government and voluntary social agencies to succor and help those who are ill or unfortunate. We are learning better all the time to respect the rights of individuals and the dignity of every human being.

Some of these things are not understood abroad because too frequently those who represent us abroad are in the business of trade or politics and are not well schooled in the advances we have made in human relations, or they fail to practice those which we have learned in the years of our growth and struggle. What we must do is to further improve our human relations at home to advance the welfare of all men, and by our example to show the rest of the world that our ideology has a spiritual and human content which drives men forward to new successes and achievements for the benefit of a whole society.

It is futile to preach this doctrine abroad unless each of us feels it deeply at home. On this conviction we can then add to our contributions of dollars, commodities and weapons a new note of understanding for people everywhere—an understanding that is basic to the social work which you practice and that is certain to be an important element in the establishment of world peace.

With these goals in mind and with my firm wish for your success in these meetings and afterwards, I bid you dedicate your thought and your energies to strengthening your work, and the principles that guide you so that we may in turn assist others and increase the effectiveness of our relations with nations beyond the seas.

Because the work you are doing is so important it must be done constantly better. I hope your sessions here prove to be helpful to all of you in achieving the better methods, the better coordination of efforts, the better emphasis and above all the better understanding on the part of the people and yourselves as to the responsibilities and limitations of the welfare services, public and private.

Again I welcome you cordially to Illinois—and I warn you that if you wait another sixty years before you return I shall never forgive you. I shall refuse to welcome you the next time—even if I'm asked!

HAMPDEN-SYDNEY COLLEGE COMMENCEMENT, HAMPDEN-SYDNEY, VIRGINIA,
June 9

MY GREAT-GRANDFATHER, Dr. Green, who was President of Hampden-Sydney College just one hundred years ago, has always interested me. He studied at Yale, at the Princeton Theological Seminary and in Europe. He was a college president in the great nineteenth century tradition—a classical scholar, an ordained and gifted minister of the Presbyterian Church, an intellectually and spiritually whole man. I often wish I had inherited more of his characteristics! He once wrote in a letter to his daughter, my grandmother, that "the love of applause is essentially an unhealthy stimulus to the human mind." And here I am a politician!

So you will see that in spite of the interval of a hundred years, I do not feel altogether a stranger at Hampden-Sydney, and I am deeply grateful for the honor and the opportunity you have afforded me to come to the home of my ancestors here in Virginia.

But what am I to say to you who have completed your undergraduate work that has not been said to you before and better said a hundred times? Well, obviously, there is nothing, or very little, that I can say or that you will remember, on this important symbolic day in your lives, unless perhaps it's this bit of nonsense that I spied in a newspaper last week:

> Gentlemen of the graduating class: Seldom have I looked into so many young faces expressing complete perplexity. From your countenances there leaps the question, 'Now what?' My answer may be wrong, but take consolation from the fact I am not sending it collect.

You are stepping forth into a world under conditions in which even a compass, barometer, non-skid tires, a self-winding watch and a rugged constitution are no longer dependable.

These are curious times. The world seems mad, your country acts queerly, leaders of city, state, nation and the continents behave weirdly. Who am I to get critical if you, too, show psychopathic symptoms?

These are grave times. This summer you will be subject to the special peril of political convention speeches. If you have jobs as lifeguards and are under water during July it will be a break.

You are graduating in a period of war, inflation, wrong answers, potato shortages, economic chaos and the twenty cent cup of coffee. Nothing is certain in the immediate future but nuttier popular songs sung more loudly, higher taxes, longer commercials and continued assurances from Washington that all is well.

One thing is in your favor today: you are young, possess all your hair and have charm. This makes you eligible at least for a job of some kind in television. If you are beyond question not quite bright you can become government economists.

Hail and farewell! Also good luck and plenty of aspirin. May you never refuse to testify on the ground it may incriminate and degrade you. The world is your oyster. Don't settle for clam bisque.

Somehow that piece reminds me that the annual admissions to mental hospitals equal the graduations from college. But maybe it's as good a text as any, because it *is* a strange, disordered, anxious world you face. Yet doesn't the world always look that way on commencement day? Isn't the old order always changing? Are not people always yearning vaporously for the good old days when everything seemed more certain and secure? But those days were never as good as they seemed. And this, in spite of all the sin, sickness, disorder and head cracking problems we face, seems to me an exciting, exhilarating time to be alive. The important thing is to be alive, to be a part, a positive, active, participating part of your generation.

Let me talk to you a few minutes, tiresomely I'm afraid, about your turbulent era.

There are many interpretations of the crisis but there is no disagreement that this is a conclusive period in human history, "an age between the ages." The era of absolute national sovereignty is over but the age of international order with political instruments powerful enough to regulate the relations of nations and to adjust their differing desires is not yet born. The era is past in which a technical and industrial civilization could be counted on to regulate itself. But the age in which justice is achieved within each nation, and yet freedom maintained, by a wise and responsible regulation, is still ahead. This is a period of transition and as John C. Calhoun some time ago reminded us: "An age of transition must always necessarily be one of uncertainty, confusion, error, and wild and fierce fanaticism."

A physician said recently to a patient: "What you need is a few months vacation—on another planet." Maybe so! But none of us will get that vacation! We will stay right here and with the help of Providence make some sense out of this turmoil.

We see pretty clearly what ought to be done to bring order and peace, but somehow mankind lacks the capacity to do it. At the start of this century it was widely assumed that if enough people realized what needed to be done, it would be done. Your fathers were taught that peace could be confidently expected if only enough people were convinced the world was really one, and that world wars would cease once their horror was widely advertised. Now, after two world wars, a cold war, a half war and who knows what to come, we are tempted to forget that mankind will certainly one day find the moral resources and political instruments adequate for a wholesome communal life on a world-wide scale. Our task is to pick up the problem in the form which history presents it to us, and push the answer as far as our fingertips can reach, counting on those who come after us to carry it further.

Our problem, your problem, is peace, peace in the community of the world—a community crowded with people of great diversity of views, of aspiration, of wealth. Even before the close of the last war, most of our people had seen clearly that isolation from the rest of the community was no answer to the problem of our security in this contracted world. In launching the United Nations organization they evidenced their decision that the safest way to avert further discord in the family was to discourage the aggressor before he gets started, by organized community action. This conviction was reinforced as the threat of the Soviet Union became clearer. And because we are so rich and powerful, no combination of free states is adequate to meet the challenge that does not include us, and we cannot meet that challenge alone. We cannot hope to save ourselves without saving a good part of the world as well. Isolation has not lost all its emotional appeal, but it has lost its intellectual respectability.

In a very brief time America has been thrust into a position of enormous responsibility. Indeed, anyone who understands what is now required of our country finds himself saying, "Can we do it?" This first reaction of awe and humility is probably sound. Whoever starts in that mood has some realistic comprehension of what is asked of us, and takes our monstrous responsibilities seriously.

But if we start with doubts, we better not stop there. Fortunately most of us don't. And your job will be to see how well America can exercise responsibility by helping her exercise it.

This rivalry with Russia is not the source of all of our problems. The present crisis in world affairs has deep origins in the social and economic changes of our century, in the revolution in communication and transport that has poured the entire planet into one container, in the development of new and ever more lethal weapons, in the decline in previously accepted standards and values. But the depth and severity of the crisis does not alter the immediate difficulties. Unless we handle the challenge of the Soviet Union wisely we cannot guide the world toward more enduring international arrangements.

How then is the world going to handle its social, economic, and political problems? Obviously they are going to be handled on some basis. The nations will live together in one fashion or another. Is it to be on the basis of domination and subordination—in accordance with Soviet precedents? Or is it to be on the basis of consideration and adjustment of mutual interests—in loyalty to the central convictions of democracy? Is the world of tomorrow to be run by a nation that demands a monopoly of power, or will we stand resolute and keep open the possibility of a cooperative world?

Our statesmen are absorbed these days in developing military strength to deter attack because it does not pay. We have accepted the appalling cost of rearmament and military assistance as the immediate condition of security. But the mere existence of power in the free world can only lead to an uneasy security. The arms race must end before it ends us. Power is not peace and we need to do a lot more thinking about what is required beyond the immediate necessity of strength. We correctly read the lesson of the past that a policy of weakness in this sort of world is disaster. But we have not yet seen clearly where the policy of strength is going.

Obviously full-scale war is less a way out of trouble than a way into more trouble. Our problem is to devise the means for making co-existence with a ruthless, inscrutable, tyranny tolerable. There is no escape from the perennial problem—to develop moral and political means of peaceful communal life among the nations.

We will not beat the Soviet Union except by beating them with a better idea. We can show up tyranny as a method of handling international problems by making cooperation work, at least in that part of the world in which we have influence. Free men can demonstrate that it pays to be free.

We will not get an international system for disarmament or control of atomic energy with foolproof safeguards, except by negotiation and cooperation with the Russians. Other problems cannot be successfully handled before such cooperation is possible. We do not know when our growing strength may make serious negotiation with the Soviet Union possible. We cannot be sure what fundamental changes must take place inside Russia. But we must keep the door open; we must make manifest our intention, our desire, our implacable purpose, to negotiate and to cooperate. We must not give up trying to find the means of tolerable co-existence.

And it must be abundantly clear that we are concerned not simply with our own safety but with the future of all those who work in company with us. We must continue to concert our policies with our allies. If we prove that international cooperation gets results, then the case for tyranny is further weakened.

There are a host of positive tasks for you. How to attract the allegiance of millions throughout the world who have not yet decisively rejected the false promises of Communism, particularly in the Middle and Far East. That rejection will be largely shaped by positive performance, the American performance in particular; by our ability to avoid the disruptions of depression, to guarantee equality of opportunity, to diminish prejudice and discriminatory practices, to root out corruption, to preserve freedom of thought and speech.

Shakespeare may be right when he says in Macbeth: "...security is mortals' chiefest enemy." But certainly the insecurity and anxiety of this era has taken a heavy toll. We doubt our beliefs and believe our doubts. Many of our citizens have padlocked their minds. They cannot act confidently, much less reasonably. They are submerged in irrational nightmares. They suspect their neighbors and guard their tongues. Is it possible that fear, hysteria, and witch-hunts are the ugly spawn of a century of progress, prosperity and security? Are they producing a state of society in America where it is dangerous to express an opinion. Can you imagine Thomas Jefferson afraid to express an opinion? Or Tom Paine? Or Hamilton, or

Jackson or Adams? Can you imagine these men afraid of the opinions of anyone else?

I would suggest that you remember well Algernon Sydney, a defender of religious liberty in another troublous time, and James Madison and Patrick Henry, the earliest trustees of Hampden-Sydney, and their native passion for liberty—liberty for the human mind everywhere. There is no watchword more worthy of the eternal devotion of civilized man than that.

There is trouble ahead, of course. There always is. Our need is not simply to face the somber elements of the future but also to be sure we do not let those elements obscure the future. For what lies ahead is rich with promise too.

In 1786, an English philosopher, Josiah Tucker, prophesied that Americans could never be united "under any species of government whatever." "Americans" would be, he said, "a disunited people till the end of time; suspicious and distrustful of each other, they will be divided and subdivided into little commonwealths or principalities, according to natural boundaries, by great bays of the sea, and by vast rivers, lakes and ridges of mountains." Yet look at America today! One people under one constitution.

Professor Mortimer Adler of the University of Chicago once said that it would take five hundred years for mankind to achieve the conditions of a stable peace. That is exactly the time Thomas Jefferson wrote in his *Notes on Virginia*, that it would take American civilization to get to the Pacific coast. Jefferson wrote that less than one hundred fifty years ago, and we have been on the Pacific coast for one hundred years! Perhaps Professor Adler's timetable of five hundred years can be beaten too!

It will fall to some of you, all of you more or less, to help us make the many fateful decisions about some of these problems I've mentioned, decisions that won't be made in time for you to escape the responsibility, because the conflict between liberty and tyranny is as old as human history and the decisions are continuous decisions that must be made over and over in each generation.

Of one thing I think you may be sure. Whether America stands fast now and measures up to the crisis of this critical century is a decision that is upon us. John Milton, still in college, attacked the English clergy for its failures by declaring, "The hungry sheep look up, and are not fed." The eyes, ears and hearts of a world are attuned to America. Will historians record that the hungry sheep looked up to us in 1952 and were not fed with clear, decisive leadership? As surely as we sit here today in this ancient college in the soft woods and meadows of Virginia our historic mission, however distasteful and unsought it may be, is to lead the way step by step out of this ugly, dangerous darkness into the light of peace and freedom. If we fail, if the hungry sheep look up to us and are not fed, nothing can ever erase the failure, but Western civilization will be erased.

I have kept you too long and talked too dolefully. The future, your future, is bright. We have made the right decisions in the past, we can make them again. Man is not "a naked runner lost in a storm of spears." You are more than the social animal that Seneca spoke of. You can make this world an ever better place to live in. None of us can afford to stand on the sidelines, least of all you who have jobs and wives and families ahead of you. Don't be afraid of the great, continuous decisions of your age. You are the inheritors of a great tradition born and nutured in centuries of pain and effort. You have received here its best gift—an education. Pay your debt, man the ramparts of the humane, individualist tradition—the undying faith in the eternal nobility and dignity of man. Defend it against its avowed enemies, its covert foes, and its frightened friends who would surrender it to save it

You have the components of good judgment and wise decision. Many of your decisions will be executed through the instrument of government. Of one thing now I can assure you. If responsible citizens don't make that government good government, responsive government, there will always be irresponsibles, and rascals, ready to usurp the positions and leadership which should be yours by every consideration of intelligence, integrity and patriotism. And remember that if you fail to do the chores of organized society in your township, your city, your county and your state the power of the central government will expand. As it does it beckons to the dictator, the demagogue to come and organize its vast intricacy.

For these tasks and these existing opportunities, use the equipment that God and this College have given you and that your own industry each day improves. Don't be afraid to live and to learn—to live hard and fearlessly. It is not the years in your life, but the life in your years that counts. You'll have more fun, you'll do more good, you'll get and give more satisfaction the more you know, the more you've worked and the more you've lived.

For you are on the threshold of a great adventure at a stirring time. Peril is one of the major stimulants in human history and out of dangerous situations the finest things have come. As Hotspur said, "Out of this nettle, danger, we pluck this flower, safety." Across long, evolutionary ages human advance has depended on finding in danger not paralysis and panic, but positive stimulant and incentive.

So face the perils standing erect, boldly, not sitting down complaining, yawning and waiting for a pension. For "This time like all times is a very good one, if we but know what to do with it."

MEMORIAL TO ELIJAH P. LOVEJOY, ALTON
November 9

I N MAY OF 1827, Elijah Lovejoy left his native village in the State of Maine for his first journey to his future home in the Mississippi Valley. As he came by schooner into Boston Harbor on the first leg of his long and arduous trip, he saw a frigate which had been taken from the British in the War of 1812 by the gallantry of American arms. This chance encounter moved him to write in his diary: "...as I gazed upon her and thought of the glorious achievements of my countrymen, my heart beat thick and proudly."

The youth of twenty-five who wrote those words had perhaps not yet learned what was to be borne in so hardly upon the man of thirty-five— that the glorious achievements of our countrymen are not all to be found in our military and naval annals; what he was yet to learn is that ordinary living affords many occasions for men to dare greatly, to live dangerously, and even to die nobly.

A decade from the time Elijah Lovejoy set out in such exuberant spirits to live and work in the great new Middle Country, such an occasion came to him. And, as he met it —bravely, directly, unyieldingly—so today do our hearts, in his phrase, "beat thick and proudly" as we meet to remember the first martyr to the freedom of the press, the freedom not just to denounce heretics, but to pronounce heresies, the freedom to say lawful but unpopular things.

To many of his contemporaries it must have seemed that Lovejoy's cause had ended in defeat. His own life was gone, his family stricken with grief and destitute, his hearse and his memory reviled by those who wanted no talk of human freedom to disturb their complacency and the existing order of things.

Lovejoy embraced a great idea in an early and perilous stage of that idea's development. And that is usually dangerous, particularly when the idea is a new idea, disturbing to existing institutions, habits and prejudices. His idea was that the enslavement of black by white was wrong and should be ended. That was a very radical idea and much more blood was to flow, the lives of millions more were to be wrecked, before that idea was to prevail.

But the measure of Lovejoy's triumph is to be found in the fact that only a quarter of a century was required to establish it as the law of the land. And across this scene of Lovejoy's death there fell, some twenty years later, the shadow of the tall, gaunt man who was to be the instrument to do this work. For not far from the plaque we dedicate today is the marker commemorating the last of the Lincoln-Douglas debates, held here in Alton on October, 1858.

Elijah Lovejoy, however, served a greater cause than that of the abolition of negro slavery. And it was his devotion to this cause which we will remember long after the struggle over the abolition of slavery has been all but forgotten.

This greater cause was the right—and the duty—of the individual to speak out for the truth. I make the reference to "duty" advisedly because that was the way Lovejoy thought of it. To his fellow citizens of Alton in meeting assembled to protest the turmoil provoked by his outspokenness, he said something like this:

"I am impelled to the course I have taken because I fear God. As I shall answer to my God in the great day, I dare not abandon my sentiments, or cease in all proper ways to propagate them. I can die at my post but I cannot desert it."

There are many vigorous and powerful statements of the right to be permitted to speak freely, but I know of none more moving. And in these days of clamorous and jostling assertion of rights and privileges, it is sobering to be reminded by these words of duties as well as rights.

Lovejoy saw the problem in terms of what he felt obliged to say, not merely of what he might be entitled to say. The distinction is an important one; and only those who observe the one as well as claim the other serve the cause of truth.

Human character being what it is, heroes in the classic mould of Elijah Lovejoy are rare. Of such stuff were the martyrs made. Neither is it given to many to see the truth in human affairs with the clarity and depth of Lovejoy's crusading conviction. But we can have confidence in the ultimate triumph of truth, and in the certainty that our fellow men will seek it out and follow it if only they can hear and speak and sift the true and false in untrammeled peace.

Some of the residents of Alton did not have that confidence in 1837. Some of our fellow citizens of America do not have that confidence today.

One of the greatest and wisest of living Americans, speaking in the detachment and wisdom of his retirement from the bench, found words for his countrymen not long ago when he said: "I believe that that community is already in the process of dissolution where each man begins to eye his neighbor as a possible enemy, where non-conformity with the accepted creed, political as well as religious, is a mark of disaffection; where denunciation without specification of backing, takes the place of evidence; where orthodoxy chokes freedom of dissent, where faith in the eventual supremacy of reason has become so timid that we dare not enter our convictions in the open lists to win or lose."

The American conviction could not find a more accurate statement than this by Judge Learned Hand. It has been the American conviction from the beginning that men are only free when they respect each others' freedom.

It is said that religious creeds are written to mark the graves where heresies lie buried. Besides commemorating the birth and death of an editor who had to proclaim the truth at all costs, it seems to me we are also dedicating a stone to mark the grave of a heresy. It is a common heresy and its graves are to be found all over the earth. It is the heresy that says you can kill an idea by killing a man, defeat a principle by defeating a person, bury truth by burying its vehicle. Man may burn his brother at the stake, but he cannot reduce truth to ashes; he may murder his fellow man with a shot in the back, but he does not murder justice; he may even slay armies of men, but as it is written, "truth beareth off the victory."

It is fitting that we dedicate this memorial to Elijah Lovejoy here in Alton, as a constant reminder of our eternal battle. For we fight not against flesh and blood, but we fight, in the long run, against the spiritual enemies of Man himself.

It is also the genius of American freedom that we admit our mistakes, even as we confess our sins. So today we confess our sins even as we reaffirm our faith, that "Truth crushed to earth, will rise again," that a people, under God, can have a new birth of freedom, that every age needs men who will redeem the time by living with a vision of things that are to be.

I am proud to have a part in the dedication of this reminder of the death place of a man who went all the way for what he believed.

APPENDIX

The following is a list of public addresses delivered by Governor Stevenson during his term of office. No speeches from his 1952 Presidential campaign are included.

Radio broadcast of an Address to the American Legion at Lincoln's Tomb, Springfield, February 12, 1949

Merchants and Manufacturers Club, Chicago, March 17, 1949

Civic Reception for Bishop O'Connor, Springfield, March 18, 1949

Jefferson-Jackson Day Dinner, Springfield, March 31, 1949

Jefferson-Jackson Day Dinner, Chicago, April 7, 1949

Budget Message to the 66th General Assembly, Springfield, April 19, 1949

Remarks at Lloyd Lewis' Grave, Libertyville, April 23, 1949

Radio Report to the People of Illinois, Springfield, April 19, 1949

Innauguration of D.W. Morris as President of Southern Illinois University, Carbondale, May 5, 1949

Installation of President Leslie Holmes at Northern Illinois University, DeKalb, May 13, 1949

Reception for the French "Merci" Friendship Train, Springfield, May 19, 1949

Radio Report to Illinois, Springfield, May 23, 1949

Special Message to the 66th General Assembly, Springfield, June 2, 1949

Commencement Address at Illinois College, Jacksonville, June 12, 1949

Radio Report to Illinois on the Conclusion of the 66th General Assembly, Springfield, July 7, 1949

Soldiers and Sailors Reunion, Salem, July 28, 1949

Summer Encampment of the Illinois National Guard, Camp McCoy, Wisconsin, July 31, 1949

American Legion Convention, Chicago, August 5, 1949

Governor's Day State Fair, Springfield, August 18, 1949

Unveiling of a Statue of Benjamin Franklin, Springfield, September 8, 1949

Cook County Democratic Picnic, Chicago, September 11, 1949

Litchfield Chamber of Commerce, September 27, 1949

State Federation of Labor Convention, Springfield, September 28, 1949

Conference on the Reorganization of State Government, Chicago, September 29, 1949

Illinois Chamber of Commerce, Chicago, October 7, 1949

Illinois Association of Secondary School Principals, Champaign, October 11, 1949

Inland Daily Press Association, Chicago, October 18, 1949

Dedication of State Street Bridge, Rockford, October 21, 1949

New York Herald Tribune Forum, New York, October 24, 1949

Introduction of Jawaharal Nehru to the Chicago Council on Foreign Relations, October 26, 1949

Conference on Juvenile Delinquency Prevention, Chicago, November 4, 1949

Illinois Agricultural Association, Chicago, November 16, 1949

Decatur Association of Commerce, November 30, 1949

Illinois Retail Farm Equipment Association, Peoria, December 3, 1949

State CIO Convention, Chicago, December 9, 1949

Citizens' Committee for the Hoover Report, Washington, D.C., December 12, 1949

Illinois Manufacturers Association, Chicago, December 13, 1949

Conference on Industrial Safety, Chicago, December 14, 1949

American Legion Dinner, Princeville, December 19, 1949

Jackson Day, Springfield, Missouri, January 7, 1950

American Jewish Federation of Chicago, January 19, 1950

Centre College, Danville, Kentucky, February 7, 1950

American Legion Pilgrimage, Springfield, February 12, 1950

Coal Strike Settlement Statement, Springfield, March 1, 1950

Jefferson-Jackson Day, Indianapolis, March 4, 1950

Masaryk Centennial, Chicago, March 4, 1950

Dedication of New Sinai Temale, Chicago, March 5, 1950

Illinois Housing Day, Chicago, March 13, 1950

Philadelphia Bulletin Forum, March 22, 1950

Illinois PTA Congress, Chicago, April 20, 1950

Statement on Rent Control to a Senate Committee, Washington, D.C., April 25, 1950

Insurance Federation of Illinois, Chicago, April 28, 1950

Civil Service Assembly, Springfield, May 2, 1950

Jefferson Jubilee, Chicago, May 15, 1950

Governor's Highway Safety Council, Springfield, May 17, 1950

Dedication of Stevenson Recreation Field, Farmersville, May 28, 1950

Commencement Address, Western Illinois University, Macomb, June 1, 1950

Dedication of McAdams Highway, Alton, June 4, 1950

President's Conference on Industrial Safety, Washington D.C., June 6, 1950

Illinois Governor's Day, Mooseheart, June 11, 1950

Commencement Address, University of Illinois, Urbana, June 18, 1950

Message to Special Session of the 66th General Assembly, Springfield, June 19, 1950

Memorial Hospital Dedication, Fairfield, June 25, 1950

Fiscal Year End Report, July 3, 1950

150th Anniversary of Indiana Territorial Organization, Vincennes, Indiana, July 4, 1950

Address to 33rd Division National Guard, Camp McCoy, Wisconsin, July 9, 1950

Lions International Convention, Chicago, July 16, 1950

Centennial of St. Anne, July 28, 1950

First International Trade Fair, Chicago, August 7, 1950

AFL Executive Council, Chicago, August 10, 1950

Governor's Day, Illinois State Fair, Springfield, August 17, 1950

Address to 44th Division Illinois National Guard, Camp McCoy, Wisconsin, August 20, 1950

American Legion State Convention, Chicago, September 8, 1950

Nauvoo Grape Festival, September 9, 1950

League of Women Voters, Springfield, September 15, 1950

American Bar Association on Criminal Law, Washington, D.C., September 19, 1950

Corn-ival Celebration, Streator, September 22, 1950

Murphysboro Centennial Celebration, September 29, 1950

Rantoul U.N. Festival, October 1, 1950

American Prison Association, St. Louis, October 9, 1950

Century of Health Progress, Quincy, October 14, 1950

Chicago Historical Society Gettysburg Address Exhibit, November 19, 1950

University of Chicago Law School Alumni Association, November 21, 1950

Dedication of Highway Bridge over Little Wabash, Carmi, November 24, 1950

American Public Welfare Association, Chicago, December 1, 1950

Radio Address on Gateway Constitutional Amendment, December 7, 1950

Roundtable on Tax and Fiscal Policy, Chicago, December 8, 1950

Radio Report to the People, January 11, 1951

Highway Police Dedication Program, Springfield, January 25, 1951

Northwestern University's 100th Anniversary, Evanston, January 28, 1951

Budget Message to General Assembly, April 10, 1951

Radio Report to the People, April 22, 1951

Dedication of the Training School for Boys, St. Charles, May 6, 1951

Dedication of Mt. Vernon Tuberculosis Sanitarium, May 13, 1951

Veterans Mental Hospital, Danville, May 20, 1951

Address on the State Highway Program, Springfield, June 8, 1951

Commencement, University of Illinois Professional Schools, Chicago, June 15, 1951

Groundbreaking for Lake Meadows Housing Development, Chicago, 1951

Veterans of Foreign Wars, State Convention, Springfield, July 13, 1951

Radio Report to the People on the 67th General Assembly, July 15, 1951

Governor's Day, State Fair, Springfield, August 16, 1951

State Township Officials Association, Springfield, September 25, 1951

Round Table on Emergency Problems, Annual Governors' Conference, Gatlinburg, Tennesee, October 1, 1951

Dedication of Abbot's Children's Center, Peoria, October 8, 1951

Convention of the Illinois Federation of Labor, Springfield, October 9, 1951

Illinois Human Relations Commission, Springfield, October 11, 1951

Madison County Bar Association, October 17, 1951

National Conference of Juvenile Agencies, Chicago, October 20, 1951

Sangamon County Bar Association, Springfield, October 24, 1951

Dedication of Kewanee Armory, November 8, 1951

Radio Report to the People, November 9, 1951

Dedication of SIU Training School, Carbondale, November 16, 1951

Address at 88th Anniversary of the Dedication of the Gettysburg Battlefield, Gettysburg, Pa., November 19, 1951

Message on West Frankfort Mine Disaster, December 28, 1951

Radio Report to the People, January 10, 1952

Robinson Chamber of Commerce, January 15, 1952

Address to the National Urban League, New York, January 21, 1952

Banquet for the Fourth Degree Knights of Columbus, Chicago, February 24, 1952

Citizens Schools Committee, Chicago, March 3, 1952

Jackson Day Dinner, Springfield, March 20, 1952

Springfield Association of Life Underwriters, April 2, 1952

Statement on Presidential Candidacy, April 16, 1952

New York State Democratic Committee Dinner, New York, April 17, 1952

Dallas Council on World Affairs, April 22, 1952

Oregon Democratic State Committee, Portland, May 1, 1952

Norwegian National League and Independence Day, Chicago, May 17, 1952

Dedication of Community House and Jewish Temple, Chicago, May 18, 1952

Dedication of Northern Illinois University's Parson Library, Dekalb, May 18, 1952

McKendree College Commencement, Lebanon, May 20, 1952

Conference of Social Workers, Chicago, May 25, 1952

Roosevelt College Founder's Dinner, Chicago, May 28, 1952

Springfield Manufacturer's and Employer's Association, May 29, 1952

Hampden-Sydney College Commencement, Virginia, June 9, 1952

Commencement, John Marshall Law School, Chicago, June 21, 1952

Radio Report to the People, July 1, 1952

Governor's Day, State Fair, Springfield, August 14, 1952

Dedication of Memorial to Elijah P. Lovejoy, Alton, November 9, 1952

Philip Murray Memorial Dinner, Atlantic City, New Jersey, December 3, 1952

Address to Joint Session of the 68th General Assembly, January 7, 1953

Final Radio Report to the People, January 7, 1953